Jar Spells *for the* Spiritual Witch

A Step-by-Step Guide to Creating Your Own Spells for Protection, Prosperity, and Peace

MAREN ASHFORD

For privacy reasons, some names, locations, and dates may have been changed.

This book is intended for informational and spiritual purposes only. It does not constitute medical, legal, or psychological advice, and results from any practices described cannot be guaranteed. Readers are encouraged to use their own judgment and discretion.

Book Cover Design and Interior Formatting by 100Covers.

Published by: ER Creative Publishing
Seattle, Washington, USA
ISBN:

Table Of Contents

Introduction

My own path with jar magic began in my grandmother's herb-scented kitchen, where everyday Mason jars held both preserved vegetables and precious magical workings. My grandmother taught me that magic wasn't something separate from daily life but rather a practical art woven into our most ordinary moments. Those early lessons revealed how mindfully combining natural elements within a consecrated space could manifest real change in both the physical and spiritual realms.

For centuries, people across the world have placed their hopes and intentions inside jars, turning a simple act into a spiritual practice. From medicine bundles and sealed bottles to canopic jars and singing bowls, the power of contained magic speaks to something universal in us. These diverse traditions share timeless wisdom that, when understood, helps us create profound magical practices for our modern lives.

Over years of travel and study, I've seen how different cultures use contained magic in daily life. Each tradition shows how intention shapes the physical world in a small, held space. Across these practices, there's a shared understanding that a well-prepared container can be a powerful tool for change.

In this book, we'll look at jar magic as both a craft and a spiritual practice. You'll find practical steps alongside the reasons why these spells work. We'll cover how to choose the right jar and ingredients, how to work with natural cycles, and how to dispose of your spells when they're done, all in a way that blends the practical with the spiritual. Whether you're new to spellcraft or have been practicing for years, my goal is to give you clear, down-to-earth guidance for making jar spells that work. This isn't about following strict rules. It's about building a deeper connection with yourself, the world around you, and the unseen threads that run through our lives.

By crafting jar spells we can protect, heal and reinforce our desires. Jar magic allows us to take our personal energy and bottle it, giving our intentions a more potent and lasting life.

As you begin this journey, remember that every jar spell is an act of creation, a chance to step into your own power. Each one you make draws on ancient traditions while reflecting your unique spirit. Let this book guide you as you explore the power of jar magic, helping you set clear intentions and shape rituals that fit your life today.

CHAPTER 1

The Sacred Vessel

Jar magic starts with something simple: the container itself. Before you think about spells or ingredients, it's the jar that matters. Across cultures and centuries, people have trusted these vessels to hold hopes, protect sacred items, and create change, from Egyptian canopic jars to the sealed pottery of medieval alchemists. A jar isn't simply a container. It's a small, held space where your intentions can take shape. The spiritual power of jar magic lies in its ability to create a defined sacred space where magical intentions can be focused and grow. Like seeds planted in fertile soil, magic housed within a properly prepared sacred space has room to manifest and bloom. This containment serves both practical and spiritual purposes - physically holding the magical ingredients while energetically concentrating their power.

My daughter's first jar spell was made in our kitchen to help with her insomnia. Together we filled a cobalt blue bottle with moonlight water, lavender, rose petals, and skullcap to invite calm and rest. We set our intention for peaceful, worry-free sleep and sealed it with wax. That bottle became both a tool for rest and a reminder of how powerful clear intention can be. In the chapters ahead, we'll delve deep into the alchemical principles that make this practice effective, exploring both ancient wisdom and modern applications. We'll learn how to select, cleanse, and consecrate our materials, and how to work with their inherent properties to enhance our magical intentions. Through this understanding, you'll develop not knowledge, but a genuine relationship with the magical tools you use in your practice.

Like Rory, who still keeps that first sleep jar as a teaching tool, we'll discover that the most powerful magic comes from understanding both the practical and spiritual aspects of our craft. This foundation will serve as the cornerstone for all the magical work we'll explore together, helping you develop a deep and meaningful practice that honors both ancient traditions and your own magical intuition.

The color of your jar and wax can enhance the magic within.

Blue – Water, relaxation, loyalty, peacefulness, inspiration, trust

Red – Fire, passion, courage, assertiveness, strength

Orange – Creativity, abundance, confidence, positivity, freedom

Yellow – Happiness, friendship, inspiration, learning, knowledge

Green – Fertility, change, abundance, luck, healing, peace & prosperity, money

Purple – Spirituality, power, magic, enlightenment, Wisdom, imagination, overcoming

Pink – Acceptance, beauty, compassion, self-love, nurturing, kindness, affection

Brown – Endurance, stability, balance, security, harmony

Black – Force, protection, anti-hex, spell breaking, stability, dignity

Grey – Shielding, self-defense, neutrality

White/ clear – All purpose, purity, serenity, truth, peace

Remember, while the color can enhance your jar magic, ultimately your intention is what makes the spell work.

People have used special containers in spiritual practice for thousands of years. From the sealed jars of ancient Egypt to the ritual bowls of South America, these objects were used for more than storage; they helped people mark what mattered and give form to their intentions.

In ancient Peru, people used ritual vessels to connect with the spirit world. I've always been fascinated by the Whistling Bowls of the Andes (Huacos Silbadores), ceramic jars with two chambers that made eerie sounds when filled with water. Shamans used them to guide spiritual journeys. The bowls often showed animals or mythological figures, turning each one into a story. In medieval Europe, alchemists treated tools like the athanor and crucible as sacred spaces for transformation. I see the same idea in many spiritual practices today: when the space feels right, the energy can take shape.

People have used jars and containers in magic for centuries. In 16th- and 17th-century Europe, witch bottles were filled with protective ingredients and buried near homes to keep harm away. You still see echoes of that today. Many people choose their jars with care, paying attention to the shape, size, and material to match the kind of work they want to do.

Archaeological finds show how far back these practices go. Some ritual containers still hold traces of herbs and pigments, giving us a direct link to the people who once used them. They remind us that using vessels in spiritual work is one of the oldest practices we have.

Creating a spiritual jar gives you something solid to focus your energy on. Whether you're trying to feel more grounded, sleep better or bring a bit more clarity into your day, the jar acts as a quiet reminder of what matters. It can turn vague intentions into something real.

The material you choose for your spiritual jar does more than shape its appearance—it supports your intention. Different materials carry different energies. Clay feels grounding. Glass can reflect, magnify or contain. the weight or color of a jar can affect how your spell feels and works. When you choose with care, the jar becomes more than a container—it becomes part of the magic.

Glass is often chosen for its clarity and the way it amplifies energy. Clear glass lets you see your magic taking shape, which works well for spells focused on insight or manifestation. It also brings a sense of light and openness to your practice. Blue glass feels calming and is often linked to healing. Brown glass has a grounding energy.

Metal containers bring their own qualities to magical work. Iron supports protection and banishing. Copper encourages healing and prosperity. Silver, connected to the moon, works well for emotional or intuitive spells. Metal's strength makes it useful when you need firm boundaries.

Ceramic and clay jars link you to earth energy, making them a strong choice for grounding or abundance. Their long history in traditional pottery ties your practice to older ways of working. Unglazed clay can also allow for a natural exchange between the jar and what's inside.

Wooden containers carry the energy of trees. Oak brings strength, pine clears and draws in, and cedar supports cleansing and resilience. Because wood comes from living material, it's especially useful for growth spells and anything rooted in nature.

When choosing a container, think about both practical and magical qualities. Make sure the size suits your materials and leaves room for energy to move. It should be easy to add or remove items. Most importantly, it should feel right for what you're doing. Go with what draws you in but keep the traditional meanings in mind. Glass and metal can last for years if you look after them. Wood may break down over time, which can suit magic meant to release or fade gradually.

While traditional materials each have their strengths, you can still create powerful magic with whatever's on hand. Much of magic is tied to honoring and respecting the Earth so repurposing a bottle or jar can enhance your magic. What matters is knowing the energy your container brings and choosing one that suits your purpose. The container becomes part of the spell. Its material affects how your magic takes shape and how long it lasts. When you choose with care and prepare it properly, you lay the groundwork for effective, grounded practice.

The shape of your container isn't merely decorative; it can help channel your intention and strengthen your magical focus. Some shapes encourage energy to flow outward, while others draw it inward or hold it in place. Choosing a form that aligns with your purpose can make your working more powerful. Across spiritual traditions, these shapes carry meaning that goes beyond appearance. They reflect an understanding that structure can guide energy, sharpen your focus, and support the change you're working to bring about.

Round jars often feel the most familiar. They represent wholeness and cycles, and their shape creates a steady boundary. That makes them useful for protection spells or work that needs to last. Energy flows easily within them, which helps keep things moving over time.

Shape can shift the focus of your spell. Tall jars feel more upward and outward, which suits spirit work, guidance, or anything reaching for clarity. Short, wide jars feel more grounded. They're good for protection, stability, or anything you want to anchor in your physical space.

It also helps to think about the opening. A narrow neck channels energy in one direction, which suits focused, intentional work. A wide mouth allows for more flow and exchange. That makes it a good fit for spells that are open-ended, creative, or designed to shift and grow.

Hexagonal shapes often appear in traditional vessels, mirroring patterns in nature like honeycomb. They feel balanced and rhythmic, which makes them a good fit for healing or slow, steady growth.

Shape matters. A round jar with a tight lid can help hold boundaries, especially in protection spells. A six-sided jar might work better for abundance magic, where you want flow and balance working together.

The way you place items in the jar also shapes its energy. A circle keeps things flowing, five points add protection, and spirals encourage growth and momentum. These small choices help your spell reflect what you're asking for. Since magic is closely tied to the Earth and her natural forces, choose jars that feel right to you. I often reuse jars from honey or spices or pick up bottles that catch my eye in thrift stores. Sometimes the perfect container appears when you least expect it, you just have to stay open to it. You don't need rare or antique jars; even a plain mason jar can hold powerful magic if you use it with intention. What matters most is how the shape supports your goal. Shape can affect timing too. Tall jars often slow things down, which suits longer workings. Shorter ones can help speed things up. The right shape helps your spell unfold in a way that matches your goal.

The more you work with different jars, the more you'll notice what each shape brings out. Which ones feel right for say, for love, protection, or change? Let your experience guide you.

The first thing I always do is prepare the jar. It's like clearing a space before a spell: Simple, but important. This small step helps set the tone and gives your magic the conditions it needs to grow.

Start by cleansing the container. You're wiping away any lingering energy and giving yourself a clean slate. You could rinse it with blessed water, pass it through smoke, or use sound to shift the energy inside. Each method has its own feel, so go with whatever suits you best. What matters most is that it feels intentional. That moment of care and focus sets everything in motion.

I often start with water. It's one of the simplest ways to clean a jar, and you've got options: spring water, moon water, or even tap water with a little sea salt. As you rinse it, picture washing any old energy away. The salt helps on both a magical and physical level, which is why I come back to it again and again.

Smoke works too. If I'm using rosemary or lavender, I'll burn just a small bundle and let the smoke drift over the jar. You don't need anything fancy. Go with what's local, what you have, or what feels right. It's not about the herb itself but what you bring to it.

If you can't use water or smoke, sound is another option. A bell, a singing bowl, or even your voice will do the job. Let the sound ripple through and around the jar. That vibration can shift the energy just as easily as anything else.

Once your jar is clean, you can give it a purpose. This step turns it from an everyday object into something magical. You might call on a force you trust, or you might just focus your own energy and intention. I've done both, depending on the day.

One simple way is to hold the jar and picture it glowing with light. Sometimes I press the base to the earth or pass it through incense smoke. I might warm it near a candle flame or add a drop of water. Each of these ties it to one of the elements and helps me feel like the jar is ready to hold what I'm asking of it.

Some people like to time this with the moon or other celestial events. You can, if it feels right. But really, all you need is a moment of clarity and care. That's what consecration is, making something yours and asking it to hold what matters. Once your jar is ready, take time to close the space. I like to ground any leftover energy by placing my hands on the earth or holding a stone like hematite or black tourmaline. A few steady breaths can also bring everything back into balance. This helps you feel settled, and it gives the container a calm, focused energy.

There's an old idea from alchemy that still makes sense to me: first you break things down, then you bring them back together in a new way. Solve and coagula. When we clean and prepare our tools with care, we create the right conditions for the work ahead. Whatever your spell is for, i.e., protection, prosperity, something more personal, this beginning matters. When you combine what you've learned with what feels right to you, your jars carry real strength. They're not just tools. They're part of the magic.

The sacred act of cleansing and consecrating your magical tools and workspace forms the foundation of effective jar spell craft. This ancient practice, documented across numerous magical traditions, serves two essential purposes - removing unwanted energies through cleansing and dedicating items to their spiritual purpose through consecration. Like preparing a canvas before painting or tuning an instrument before playing, these preliminary steps ensure your magical workings achieve their full potential.

Cleansing begins with understanding that all objects carry energetic imprints from their previous environments and handlers. Traditional wisdom teaches us that new tools, especially those purchased from shops or markets, require thorough cleansing before magical use[16]. This removes any residual energies that might interfere with your intentions. While ancient practitioners often had access to specific sacred herbs or locations for cleansing, modern witches can achieve powerful results through various accessible methods.

The most fundamental cleansing technique involves the use of natural elements. Running water, particularly from a natural source like a stream or spring, has long been recognized for its purifying properties[16]. However, mindfully blessed tap water can serve equally well when used with clear intention. Similarly, while traditional practices might call for specific smudging herbs like white sage, ethical you can work effectively with locally abundant herbs like rosemary or cedar or use sound cleansing through bells or singing bowls.

Alchemists knew the value of working inside a protected space. They sealed their vessels to transform one thing into another, and in magic, we do something similar. When you work within a boundary, your focus sharpens. Energy doesn't drift. You give it somewhere to go. The alchemists spoke of three key forces: Sulphur for will, Mercury for the mind, and Salt for the body. When you hold those forces in the right space, they start to interact and shift. That's when transformation happens. I often think of spell jars as modern echoes of that work: small, steady spaces that hold real potential.

A sealed container helps your magic stay clear. It keeps out distraction and lets energy build. Think of it like soil around a seed. It needs darkness and stillness to take root. Your jar offers that, not only by protecting the work but by intensifying it, like a lens bringing energy into sharp focus.

When you make a spell jar, you're not just putting ingredients together. You're creating a space where energy can shift, stretch, and grow. In a way, you're making a tiny world, one that holds your intent until it's ready to become something real.

The idea of spiritual containment works differently depending on the kind of spell. In protection work, the container acts as a barrier. It filters out harmful energy and holds the boundary. In prosperity spells, the jar behaves more like a beacon or battery. It gathers helpful energy and sends it out into the space around it.

To keep energy properly contained, you need both a physical and energetic seal. Wax or lids handle the physical part, but intention and ritual seal the energy. Together, they protect the spell until it runs its course.

The alchemists believed that transformation needs both time and a protected space. That lesson still matters today. When we seal a spell jar, we're not merely holding ingredients in place. We're setting the right conditions for the work to unfold. This reminds us not to poke or check too soon. Like any real change, magic takes time and stillness.

You can strengthen their spells by working with these old ideas about spiritual containment. Whether you want to protect, attract, or transform, the container gives your magic a focused space to grow. By using this method, we tap into a long history of magical practice while shaping it for the world we live in now.

As you practice, notice how each sealing method shapes the outcome. Which ones support your goals best? How does the space inside the jar shift the energy? By staying curious and observing what works for you, you'll deepen your understanding and strengthen every spell you craft.

Remember, the physical container matters—but it's your focused intention and ritual that create the true spiritual seal. That's what gives your magic its power.

As we close this first chapter, let's return to Rory's story. Her moment of transformation didn't come from a rare herb or perfect spell—it came from seeing her jar as sacred. That's the real magic.

You've explored how different materials, shapes, and traditions give containers their power. You've seen how spiritual sealing and preparation turn simple objects into vessels for change. And now you know: your tools don't hold ingredients—they hold intention.

What you create next will carry your signature. Let your jars speak with your intention—rooted in tradition, but entirely your own.

So before you move on, take a moment. Choose a container that speaks to you. Prepare it with care. And trust that the energy you place inside will grow into something meaningful.

CHAPTER 2

Creating Sacred Space: Preparing Your Magical Workshop & Tools

I started crafting spells at my grandmother's kitchen table, where I learned that sacred space isn't about fancy tools or rare ingredients. It begins with how you prepare. The way you choose your tools and arrange your space helps focus your energy and intention. the smallest setup — a corner of a shared flat, a windowsill, a shelf — can become a powerful place for magic when you treat it with care.

Think of your space as part of the spell. As your jars hold and shape magical energy, your workspace supports and strengthens your intentions. It doesn't need to be perfect. What matters is that you approach it with purpose and attention. When you treat your space as sacred, it becomes one — ready to hold and amplify the magic you're about to make.

My first apartment was tiny. The kitchen flowed into the main room through an archway, and my bedroom was a small space sectioned off by an open bookcase filled with colored jars and books to let light through. Finding a safe place to practice magic — without setting anything on fire or knocking over my carefully made jar spells — was a real challenge!

I eventually settled on a small cigar box, which I painted and decorated with shells and pieces of glass that gave me a sense of calm and focus. Inside I kept a scarf from my grandmother, along with candles, spoons, and crystals to support my work. I cleansed it with sage incense, wrote my intention on the inside, and covered it with light purple paper to consecrate it.

The box lived on my bookcase, where I could see it from both my bed and my favorite chair in the main room. Whenever I was ready to practice, I could simply pull it out. It wasn't fancy, but it felt grounded and full of purpose.

I've found that magic flows best in places where I feel calm, focused, and connected. You don't need a grand temple, or a room set aside just for spells. What matters is how you treat the space and the energy you bring into it. A windowsill, a patch of floor, a cleared table, all of these can become sacred if you show them care.

Pick a spot where no one will disturb you. I like to look for quiet corners or rooms with a bit of natural light, but it's about what feels right to you. Notice where in your home or garden you naturally feel at ease. Those are often the best places for this kind of work. If you're planning to use herbs or incense, make sure there's enough airflow. And think, do you have somewhere to keep your tools? Is there enough room to mix and arrange your spell jars without feeling cramped?

Once you've settled on a space, clean it. Not a rushed tidy-up, but a proper wipe-down with care and intention. As you go, stay present. You're getting your mind in the right place as well as removing dust! I've always felt that a clean space clears the way for clear thinking. It helps you settle, focus, and honor the work ahead.

Once your space feels clean to the eye and touch, it's time to shift the energy. You don't need anything fancy. I've often found that the simplest methods work best. Try ringing a bell or running a singing bowl around the edge of the room. Let the sound carry through the space. Or light a little ethically sourced sage or palo santo and let the smoke drift into the corners. If smoke isn't your thing, sprinkle a pinch of sea salt while picturing light sweeping through the air, clearing any leftover heaviness.

What really matters here isn't the tools, it's how you show up. Your focus, your mood, the care you bring to the act. That's where the power sits.

With your space cleansed, it's time to set boundaries that define it as sacred. This might mean drawing a salt circle, placing crystals at the corners, or simply visualizing a protective shield. These boundaries contain magical energy and help you shift your mindset. When you step into that space, whether that be a corner of your desk, you're entering a zone of focus, intention, and care. That mental shift can bring clarity, calm, and a stronger connection to your practice. In that first apartment, it meant placing my altar box on my little table and placing the hanky on the table anchored by my crystals at the cardinal compass points. North - Earth for grounding, South—Fire for energy and growth, East—Air for clarity, and change and West—Water for healing and emotional connections

Set up your workspace so it's both practical and meaningful. Keep the tools you use most within reach and create a layout that feels intentional and calm. Some practitioners like to place items based on traditional element directions (like placing a candle in the south to represent fire), while others simply follow their instincts. The goal is to create a space that supports your practice and feels right to you.

Choose symbols of protection and power that mean something to you. That might be a traditional sigil, a religious icon, or something much more personal, like a photo, or a shell from a place you love. I've also used my grandmothers ring and a small pumpkin my son made by painting a walnut shell orange and gluing a piece of green ribbon on top a small wooden box my husband carved from a single block and a broken little bracelet belonging to my daughter; meaningful to me and very powerful. If you need to keep things discreet, something like a small crystal or a plant can still hold weight. What matters is that it feels anchored in your energy.

Try to keep your space feeling energetically clear. You might cleanse it with each new moon, at the start of the week, or whenever things feel a little off. Some people follow the seasons; others stick to the moon cycle. I think it's more important to find your own rhythm and return to it. It doesn't have to be dramatic, what counts is your presence.

Your workspace will change as you do. That's a good thing. As your practice deepens, let your space shift and grow alongside it. Whether you've built a full altar or you're using the corner of your kitchen table, hold on to what matters: intention, care, and clarity.

With time and attention, your workspace becomes more than a place you practice. It becomes part of the work itself. An ally. A witness. A quiet reminder of the path you're on.

To make jar spells that work for you, start with a few tools that feel both useful and personal. In older traditions, people treated their magical tools as part of themselves. I still do. When I pick something up, I want to know it supports what I'm doing and helps direct my focus.

The jar is the heart of the work. I like using glass or ceramic because they're sturdy and hold energy well. Clear jars let you see what's going on inside, which can be helpful if your spell is something you'll revisit. Colored jars are lovely too. For example, I like to use green if I'm drawing in money, blue when I need calm and black when I want protection. Go with what fits your spell and what seals tightly. You're holding energy here, after all.

Then there are herbs and crystals. These carry their own long histories. You don't need to spend a fortune or track down rare things. I've used basil from my kitchen for protection and prosperity, and lavender when I've needed peace. What matters isn't how fancy your ingredients are, it's how you work with them: the energy you bring, and the story you tell with each layer you add.

Crystals can lift the energy of your spell and help you direct it. I often reach for clear quartz when I want something that covers all bases, whereas black tourmaline is the one I go to for protection. Green aventurine brings in abundance. Rose quartz feels soft and loving, good for healing or anything to do with the heart. A small stone, if charged with care, can hold more power than you'd expect.

You'll also want something to write with, a scrap of paper and whatever pen you have nearby. That's enough to shape a thought into something real. Let go of the idea that you need special ink or parchment. The act of writing it down, that's where the shift starts.

To seal the spell, I like to use a candle. The wax closes the jar, and the flame sparks the work into motion. I sometimes choose a color that fits the mood of the spell, such as white for clarity, green for growth, red when there's fire behind what I want. But honestly, a plain white candle has never let me down. What makes it work is what I bring to it.

You can make your jar spells more personal by adding items that mean something to you: coins, seeds, salt, or anything that feels charged with memory or intention. A button from your grandmother's sewing kit might hold more weight than a polished charm from a shop. Trust what pulls you in.

You don't need a long list of tools. But the ones you do use need your care. I keep mine clean and separate from my everyday things. Even if it's just a small box on a shelf, it helps to know that space is for magic alone.

Some tools will speak to you more than others. That's normal. Follow the ones that feel alive in your hands. You're not trying to copy someone else's setup, you're building something real and personal, rooted in the old ways but shaped by your own rhythm.

I've always found salt to be one of the simplest, strongest ways to clear old energy. Bury your tools in it overnight, then pour the used salt into running water or scatter it outside with care. Sunlight and moonlight work too. I lean toward the full moon, but you don't have to get the timing perfect. What matters is that you show up with focus.

Once your tools feel clear, take a moment to dedicate them. I like to lay mine out with something for each of the elements: salt, a candle, a bit of water, and breath or incense. As I touch each item, I speak to it. I tell it what it's for and what I need it to help me with. This isn't about ceremony for the sake of it. It's about connection.

If it feels right, anoint your tools with oil or carve in a small symbol. Keep them in a place that feels safe and separate. When things start to feel flat or heavy, take the time to cleanse them again. I often do this on the full moon, but you'll find your own rhythm. That regular care makes a difference. It keeps your tools sharp, and your practice steady.

Although I usually prefer moonlight and salt, I turned to a different practice during the Covid pandemic. I spent time in my garden, leaving my tools in the fresh air and bright sunlight, it felt right for that moment, so that's what I did. Don't be afraid to adapt your practice; let your intuition and spirit guide the way.

Creating a strong boundary is one of the most important steps in jar spell work — and in any serious spell casting. Think of it as building a safe container for your magic: it holds what matters and keeps out what doesn't. For me, setting a boundary around my workspace feels like putting up a sturdy fence. Light and air can pass through, and small, harmless creatures are welcome, but anything harmful is kept out. You don't need rare herbs or complicated rituals to create strong boundaries. What matters is knowing what you want to protect and choosing tools that feel right to you.

I like to place protective jar spells around my space. They function as quiet guardians, marking the edges and holding the energy in place. You can follow old traditions for where to put them or simply trust your sense of where things feel vulnerable.

A simple jar might hold black tourmaline to absorb tension, sea salt to clear the air, and rosemary to keep harm away. Practitioners have used these ingredients for generations, and you can find them easily. If you don't have tourmaline, you can use obsidian or a smooth black pebble instead, if you set the intention clearly. And rosemary from the shop or garden works as well as wild sprigs, provided you handle it with care.

To make a simple boundary jar:

- Start with a clean jar. Blue or black are traditional, but translucent glass works if you charge it with purpose.
- Add your chosen items one by one, thinking about what each one does:
    - ▷ Black or sea salt to ground and clear
    - ▷ Herbs like rosemary, bay, or lavender to keep harm away
    - ▷ Stones like tourmaline, obsidian, or hematite to hold the line
    - ▷ A scrap of paper with your intention or a sigil
- Seal the jar with black or white wax during the waning moon to help send unwanted energy out.

Place your jars where energy tends to move. I usually tuck mine into corners, on windowsills, or near the front door. If you're in a flat or a shared space, a quiet windowsill can still do the trick.

You might like to create more than one jar, each with its own focus. One could help calm racing thoughts. Another might hold you steady when you're around others. A third could protect your home. Over time, you'll get a feel for what you need and where to place it.

As you go deeper, you can add layers. Mirror shards can reflect negativity. Frankincense clears the air. A personal item—something that makes you feel safe—can anchor the spell. It's not about the number of ingredients. What counts is how well you understand what you're using and the clarity behind your intention.

These jars need care. I check mine during the waning moon or when the seasons shift. You can follow your own rhythm. What matters is showing up for the work and staying connected to the reason you began.

Boundaries should help you feel safe, not cut off. Think of them like a filter: they let good energy in and keep harmful stuff out. Like your skin or the atmosphere, they hold space while still allowing flow.

As you go, lean on your instincts. You don't need to follow rigid rules. What makes a jar powerful is how well you understand your tools and how intentionally you use them. I try to think of my spells like a painting—the colors and textures should help create the desired mood in your final piece.

Keeping your tools and ingredients in order helps your spellwork feel clearer. I always find it easier to focus when everything's where it should be. Some people say their tools hold more power when they're stored with care, and I'd have to agree. How you store your things matters. It's not solely about how long something lasts, but how it feels when you reach for it. You don't need anything elaborate. I've seen friends use old spice racks and shoeboxes, The key is to keep it simple and make it yours.

Try grouping your herbs by purpose or element. Keep them in clean, dry jars. Some people like dark glass to block the light, but I've always used clear jars in a cupboard and never had a problem. What matters is that they're fresh and easy to find.

Crystals need a little extra care. They scratch easily, so give them a soft place to rest. You could use pouches, a wooden box, or those little trays with dividers. I like to recharge mine in sunlight or a bowl of salt-water, depending on what they need.

Keep your spell tools—like your mortar and pestle, spoons, and funnels—in a space that feels like yours. Some people line a box with cloth. Others keep theirs in a drawer marked with hand-drawn symbols. However you do it, try to keep these tools separate from your regular kitchen gear. It helps them hold their own energy. I also like to keep track of what I have. A notebook works for some. Others prefer a digital doc. I jot down what each ingredient's for and when it's best to use it. Then, when I'm deep in a spell, I'm not digging around for bay leaves or trying to remember what phase the moon was in last time.

If you travel, it's worth making a small kit. A pouch or little box with your favorite ingredients means you can still do your thing, even when you're not at home. I pack enough for a simple jar spell and keep it ready to go. Store your oils in dark glass bottles with proper lids and label them clearly. A nice touch is to group them by purpose—love, cleansing, grounding—and keep them far from dry herbs to avoid spills. Roll-ons are handy when working quickly. Droppers too. But for long-term storage, I always find glass is best.

When it comes to finished spell jars, give them breathing room. Keep love jars separate from protection ones and try not to let them all pile up. A shelf works well. So do small, labelled boxes. Each jar carries its own charge. Keeping them apart helps that stay strong.

I like to keep my magical tools clean and well organized, not just physically but energetically too. You might enjoy doing the same. It's a grounding ritual in itself. Some of my friends choose to clean during the waning moon or at the start of each season. That rhythm might work for you, or you might find your own. What matters is that your space stays clear and aligned with your practice.

When your tools are easy to find and your space feels calm, your spellwork flows better. You can feel it in your body. Good organization lifts the energy in the room and makes everything click into place. As you finish setting up, pause for a moment. As you finish setting up, pause for a moment. This is a turning point. A friend of mine used to work in a tangle of tools and half-finished ideas. Bit by bit, they created a space that felt like home. You're doing that too. Every time you choose what to keep, where to place it, and how to care for it, you're shaping your path. You don't need a ritual room or a fancy altar. You only need a corner that feels yours. A shelf or a windowsill can hold real power when you treat it with care.

As your practice grows, your space will likely change with it. You might move things around, by adding new tools, or shifting your setup entirely. That's part of the journey. Stay grounded in what works for you, honor old wisdom, and keep adapting. That's how your magic stays strong.

CHAPTER 3

Chamomile, Clove, and Chaos: Finding Meaning in Magical Substitutions

One of the first things I learned about magic was this: every ingredient carries its own energy. Not in some abstract way, but in a way you can feel when you slow down and pay attention. The scent of dried lavender, the cool weight of a stone, the tingle when you hold a pinch of salt between your fingers—all these things speak to us. It's a kind of language, and learning to work with it is what brings your spells to life. With them, they carry mood and meaning. You can sense it if you stay open. Each one adds something to your spell, like a word in a sentence. When chosen with care, they shape your magic in ways that feel real.

Generations of practitioners have passed down the language of correspondences, and the idea that certain ingredients carry specific qualities. People added to it through experience, not theory. Some old recipes call for rare herbs or exotic stones. But you don't need those. You can work with what's already around you, as long as you understand how it feels and what it brings.

A friend of mine, Liam, once found himself in a tiny herb shop, clutching a recipe for a prosperity jar. It mentioned Irish moss, but the shelf was empty. He looked lost. The shop owner, an older woman with green-stained hands, asked what he was trying to do. He told her.

"It's not about the name," she said. "Irish moss is for abundance and water energy. You can get that from the seaweed down at the bay. Even thyme from your garden will work if your heart's in the right place."

That was a turning point for him. It wasn't about copying a recipe anymore. It was about listening and responding. He filled his jar with local herbs that meant something to him. That spell still stands out as one of his most powerful.

Liam's reminds me that magic isn't about getting everything perfect. It's about building a relationship: with the materials, the work, and with yourself. When you know what each ingredient brings, you can create spells that feel whole, even when the recipe's changed.

Personally, I love dragon's blood as part of a jar spell to encourage healing and protection from negative energies, harmful spirits, and unwanted influences. It also evokes a strong, earthy scent that is calming and can help you focus on your desires. But Dragon's blood isn't always available, so I have used a combination of pink salt, cinnamon sticks, and rosemary to the same end. Once you imbibe the jar and its ingredients with your intent your spell should have the same end result. In this chapter, we'll look at the qualities behind common ingredients. You'll learn how to read their energy, how they link to elements and planets, and how to follow your instincts when choosing what to use. We'll also talk about substitutions. Because magic should feel possible, not precious. The rosemary on your windowsill can hold more power than something imported in plastic. When your spell grows from where you are, it starts to reflect your life, and that's when it becomes real. The more you tune in, the more your spellwork becomes something rooted, flexible, and entirely your own.

When I first started working with spell jars, I kept coming across the four elements: Earth, Air, Fire, and Water. At first, they felt symbolic, almost abstract. But the more I practiced, the more I realized they're not just metaphors. They're living energies you can invite into your work. You don't have to follow a strict system; you can learn simply by noticing how each element feels and what it brings into your space. Each jar you make is a chance to connect with those elemental forces. They're not separate from your ingredients. They move through them. You'll start to sense which elements support your intention, and which ones need balancing. Here's how I think about them now, from my own practice:

- Air is thought, breath, movement, and messages. I call on it when I need clarity, ideas, or a change of perspective. Sometimes I use a bit of mint or lavender, or a feather I found on a walk. And sometimes it's as simple as leaving space at the top of the jar. Not for practicality, but to give the spell room to breathe.

- Fire is for energy, change, and protection. When something needs to shift, I'll reach for cinnamon, red pepper flakes, or seal the jar with candle wax to bring that fire in. It's more than heat. It's about shedding what no longer serves.

- Water carries emotion, intuition, and healing. You might feel drawn to moon water, or a shell from a beach you visited on vacation. I've used morning dew and even some of my tears before. Water helps me let go and remember who I am.

Earth is grounding, holding, building. It gives your spell something solid to root into. I use soil or herbs from the garden. Anything that brings a sense of steadiness. Earth is what I lean on when I need to feel safe.

You don't need fancy tools to work with the elements. A bell can bring Air. A handwritten note can hold more Fire than a piece of dragon's blood resin if it's charged with real intent, while a sprig of rosemary from your kitchen might carry more power than something imported. It's not about getting it right. It's about paying attention. When you feel the elements as living forces, your spellwork becomes a part of you.

I've noticed over time that certain kinds of spells lean toward certain elements. For me, protection work usually pulls in Earth and Fire. Healing jars tend to call for Water and Air. You'll find your own rhythms. The more you notice what works, the more intuitive your choices become. And remember, it's not about what something *looks like*, it's about what it *carries*. A crystal doesn't work because it's a rock. It works because its energy fits your goal. Once you understand how those energies interact with your intentions, your spell jars stop feeling like recipes and start feeling like conversations.

Jar spell magic has shifted a lot over time. It's still recognizably the same at its core, but the way we work with it has changed to suit who we are and what's around us. When I first started, I felt pressure to follow the "right" recipes. That is, ones filled with rare herbs or ingredients I'd never even seen. But I quickly learned that magic has always been about adaptation. What mattered most wasn't the exact ingredient, rather, it was what that ingredient brought to the spell. You'll come across traditional materials in old books or passed-down rituals, things like frankincense for cleansing, or garlic for protection. If you have them, wonderful. But if you don't? That's not a problem. For example, I sometimes use pine resin when I can't get frankincense. And I've used onion skins once when I didn't have any garlic. It still works because I understand what I'm asking that ingredient to do.

It's the same with herbs. Basil is a classic for prosperity and protection, but I've swapped it for bay leaves plenty of times. Lavender's lovely for calm, but I often use rosemary or chamomile instead. My point is that you don't need to copy old spells exactly. Instead stay true to their purpose by working with what you have. And it's not only herbs either. With crystals, I don't always use what's named in the spell. If I don't have green aventurine, I'll use another green stone, or even green glass. If the energy fits, and I'm working with intention, I know it will hold as much power.

For sweetening spells — anything meant to draw something in gently — honey is the traditional choice. I enjoy working with maple syrup and agave but I've been known to use a bit of jam in a pinch. Vinegar's commonly used to banish or clear, but if lemon juice or apple cider is more accessible or alive to you, then either of those choices will work just fine.

A little tip. Whenever I'm substituting, I think about three things:

- What element the ingredient connects to
- The energy or role it plays in the spell
- What it symbolizes to me

That's how I decide. For example, if a spell calls for holly and I don't have it, I might reach for pine needles instead. To me, it's still protective, evergreen, grounded in the same Earth energy.

Even with personal items, things have changed. Older spells might use hair or nail clippings. These days, I've used photos, names written on paper, even a voice memo whispered over the jar. It's still personal. Still yours.

The most powerful spells I've made didn't come from elaborate ingredients. They came from what was around me, and what felt alive in the moment. I think that's what our ancestors did too. They used what they had and handled it with care. You can do the same by letting go of the idea of perfect magic. What matters is keeping the spirit alive. When your materials reflect your life and surroundings, your spell jars become part of your rhythm.

My relationship with plants began long before I knew what jar magic was. I'd pick herbs without thinking much about it: dill to have with salmon, mint for tea. It took time before I realized each plant had a spirit, and that spirit was willing to work with me, as long as I slowed down and treated it with respect.

In magic, we don't use plants. We work with them. That shift in thinking changed everything for me. I stopped rushing and started listening. Whether I was harvesting mugwort at dusk or running my fingers through dried rosemary, I was building a relationship. Mugwort, sacred to the moon, often shows up in spells for dreams or divination. But if you don't have mugwort, that's fine. Sage or mint can do the same when you know how to listen. Angelica root is known for protection. If I don't have it to hand, try using bay or rosemary. Again, I tune in and ask: does this feel right for what I'm doing?

You don't always have to go for the showy herbs. Some of my strongest spells started with a pinch of kitchen fennel or parsley. I've learned not to underestimate the quiet ones. Star anise is a good example. It sits quietly on the spice rack, but that eight-pointed shape holds real power. It brings clarity. If I take a moment to connect, it never lets me down.

Before I place anything in a jar, I spend time with it. Sometimes I speak to the plant or hold it in my palm and wait. I'm not asking for anything at that point. I'm listening. The more I do this, the clearer the messages become.

When I gather fresh herbs, I always ask first. For example, if I'm picking from my garden, I might whisper a thank you or leave water in the soil. If I'm buying dried herbs, I still take a moment to honor where they came from. Everything has a history.

Substitutions don't need to match appearance or scent. What matters is the energy. If I'm creating a protection spell for my son, I might choose lemon balm over dill. Not because it's more traditional, but because it feels gentler and more personal. Harvest timing also makes a difference. A summer herb carries light and growth. A winter one brings stillness and depth. Try to notice those differences when you build your spells, and you'll soon understand that seasonal rhythm matters.

Try keeping a notebook and jotting down what works. I like to note which herbs I felt drawn to, which ones clashed, or which ones surprised me. This record has become one of my most useful tools, more valuable than any textbook on correspondences.

Plants are generous. They show up, again and again, when we treat them with care. And when you meet them halfway, they bring something ancient and alive into your magic, something that connects you to the land, the past, and the spell you're about to cast.

Common ingredients and their uses

- **Basil** – Love, Wealth, and counteracts fear of the unknown or change
- **Bay** – Vision, Strength, Healing, Purification
- **Blackberry** – Protection, Health, Prosperity
- **Calendula** – Protection, uplifting spirits
- **Cinnamon** – Spirituality, Healing, Protection
- **Cloves** – Spirituality, Healing, Protection
- **Dandelion** – Creativity, Courage, Bravery, Banishment, Growth and transformation
- **Fern** – Protection, Luck, Visions
- **Fruit blossoms** (cherry, apple, etc.) - Love, Happiness, Partnership
- **Hazel** – Protection, Luck, Abundance
- **Heather** – Love, Luck, Protection
- **Ivy** – Binding, Strength, Luck
- **Lavendar** – Peace, Sleep, Love
- **Lemon Balm** – Healing, Love, Comfort, Calming
- **Lilac** – protect from evil, banish evil, flirtation
- **Mint** – Healing. Abundance
- **Nutmeg** – Luck, health, wealth , power
- **Oak** – Strength, protection, life
- **Olive** – Life, light
- **Parsley** – Protection, Purification. Aphrodisiac
- **Pine** – Prosperity, protection, cleansing, banishing
- **Rose** – Love, Beauty, Confidence, Truth

- **Rosemary** – All-purpose protection, strength, Power
- **Sage** – Wisdom, healing, protection, purification
- **Star Anise** – Luck, Spiritual Energy,
- **Sunflower** – Happiness, Prosperity
- **Thyme** – Protection, Courage, Psychic power, Health
- **Vanilla** – Love, Purification, Prosperity, Abundance

Jar spell magic has shifted with time, but its heart hasn't changed. When I started out, I didn't pay much attention to how things looked or felt, I was too focused on "getting it right." I began to realize that how something smells can shape the whole energy of a spell. These details aren't just for show. They help your magic speak.

I often start with color. It's one of the simplest ways to set the tone. Red gives a spell heat and momentum. Green makes me think of growth, money, or fresh starts. White always brings a sense of protection and calm, and black helps me push things away or set strong boundaries. You'll have your own associations too. For a prosperity jar, I've used moss and a green stone, as well as golden thread or scraps of green ribbon, even a copper paperclip. You don't need rare crystals. If the color speaks to your intention, it works.

Scent adds another layer. It moves through memory before thought. The smell of lavender always brings me back to steadiness. Cinnamon wakes things up. Patchouli feels grounding, and jasmine carries this soft, magnetic pull. If you're sensitive to scent (or sharing a space with someone who is), you can still call in that energy. Sometimes I'll use a pinch of herb, or write the plant's name on a slip of paper and tuck it in. That works too. Then there's texture, something I overlooked at first.

Now, I notice how a rough crystal settles me, or how the crunch of dried herbs adds a spark of energy. I'll use salt when I need a clear boundary, soft petals when I want to soothe, or sharp bits like rosemary or broken shells when I need to hold my ground.

When you build a jar, notice how the textures work together. You might start with rough stones for grounding, then add something soft to bring comfort. That contrast helps the spell hold. And if you're working with what's on hand, trust your instincts. If the spell calls for thorns and all you have is rosemary, those brittle, pointed stems might carry the energy just fine. The act is simply about understanding what you're asking each item to do.

When you layer color, scent, and texture, your jar speaks with more clarity. Everything inside supports your intention. A love spell, for example, might use pink rose petals to soften and open, paired with a smooth piece of rose quartz to steady the energy. Each piece reinforces the others.

You're not bound to a strict list. These correspondences come from tradition, but tradition was always meant to be lived with, not memorized. The more you understand how these elements work for you, the more freedom you have to shape spells that feel honest and powerful. That's the kind of magic that lasts.

Creating your own correspondence system draws on tradition but stays personal. Your jar spells feel stronger when they reflect what matters to you. There's no need to follow fixed rules. Let your magic grow from your own experience.

The Hermetic idea that everything is connected forms the root of magical correspondences. This principle, often summed up as "as above, so below," teaches that herbs, colors, and planets share natural qualities with certain intentions. Traditional correspondence systems give you a reliable starting point. These systems have been shaped over time to help people choose ingredients with purpose. Basil draws abundance. Lavender brings peace. These meanings come from practice, not theory.

Still, effective magic goes beyond memorizing lists, it's all about intuition. The more you work with materials, the more you'll notice how they interact with your energy. Your cultural background and spiritual path also shape what feels right to you. If you can blend tradition with personal insight, your practice will become yours.

When I started building my own correspondence system, I leaned hard on books and old notes. I needed the structure of traditional meanings and trusted sources. But I also started paying attention to how things felt when I used them. That part mattered just as much. I kept a journal where I recorded both the classic associations and my own experiences — the little gut feelings, the way certain herbs worked better in some spells than others. Over time, that record became more valuable than any list I could copy. It showed me how *my* magic worked, instead of how I believed it was supposed to work.

You'll likely make swaps now and then. I do it all the time. If a spell calls for something hard to find or expensive, I think about what I already have that feels similar. I've used rosemary in place of frankincense because it felt stronger in that moment. That's what matters—not whether it's "correct," but whether it works for you.

When I'm choosing ingredients for a jar spell, I hold them for a moment, feel their energy, and check in with myself. Does this feel grounding? Uplifting? Protective? Sometimes rose quartz doesn't hit quite right, but clear quartz does. That impression is enough to guide my choice. You'll develop that sense too — and the more you trust it, the stronger your spells will feel.

One of the best ways to refine your system is to experiment. Try different combinations. Keep track of what you used, when, and how it felt. Patterns will emerge. Some pairings will work again and again. Others won't land the same way. And don't be afraid to change your mind. What worked for you six months ago might shift. Maybe your connection to an ingredient deepens, or maybe something you used to love no longer fits. That's all part of growing a living practice.

When I record my correspondences now, I include add notes on how something made me feel, what memory it brought up, or why it mattered that day, as well as the meanings. That kind of detail helps me understand not just what an ingredient *does*, but why it resonates.

The strongest systems I've seen—and the one I've built for myself—blend traditional knowledge with lived experience. They give you something to lean on, but they leave space to evolve. When your spellwork grows out of that kind of practice, it becomes more effective, and most importantly it becomes more *yours*. That's what gives it staying power.

CHAPTER 4

Where the Moon Leads

The natural rhythms of the earth run through all magic. They shape the energy behind each spell, whether we notice it or not. When you start tuning in, that is, watching the moon, or feeling the seasons shift, you give your jar spells something steady to rest on. A pulse. A pattern. The same one our ancestors once followed when they looked to the sky before planting seeds or lighting candles. Each phase of the moon brings a different kind of energy. The waxing moon helps things grow and gather, while the full moon is bold and brilliant for manifesting. The waning moon, on the other hand, is better for letting go and the dark moon, quiet and still, means it's time to rest and reflect.

The moon, however, isn't the only guide. There's energy in the light at dawn, the tilt of the year and the hush before sleep. The more you move with those shifts, the more natural your magic begins to feel. You're not copying tradition. You're stepping into something older. Something that's been humming beneath our feet for a long time.

A friend of mine, Emma, started paying attention to the moon when she was building her jar spells. She noticed how the timing changed the feel of them. One evening, under a waxing crescent, she made a jar for career growth. She used mint, green aventurine, citrine, and sealed it with golden wax. A few weeks later, she got a promotion, and three new clients. That jar worked. The timing fit. And she felt it. From then on, she planned her spells with more care. No strict calendar. No rules. She simply watched and listened while letting her practice grow in a way that made sense in her life. Her jars became more than spells. They became part of her rhythm. Emma's story reminds me how easy it is to lose touch. We wake to alarms, not sunlight. We scroll through days without noticing the sky. But those deeper rhythms are still there. When you start to feel them—really feel them—you bring something richer into your work.

In this chapter, we'll look at traditional timings and how they link to jar spells. You'll learn how to adapt them to your life. Candlelight or lunch break. Big rituals or five quiet minutes. You don't need to follow every step. You just need to find what fits and let your practice grow from there.

Working with the moon changed everything for me. Once I started aligning my jar spells with its phases, things began to click into place. I realized I didn't have to do things perfectly, I just needed to tune in. The moon already offers a rhythm. When I follow that flow, my spells feel more alive.

I always begin with the Dark Moon, sometimes called the New Moon. The sky is empty then, and that emptiness feels like a fresh canvas. That's when you can set new intentions or quietly release what you've outgrown. If I'm doing a spell to reset something in my life—my energy, a relationship, an old habit—this is the moment I like to do it.

Then the moon begins to grow. The Waxing Crescent is when I focus on drawing things toward me, like confidence or hope. It's a soft, building energy. A few days later, the First Quarter arrives and brings this strong, push-forward feeling. That's when I like to do spells that help me move through obstacles or make a decision I've been putting off. The Waxing Gibbous comes next, and I always feel a sense of fullness building. If I'm working on prosperity, this is the sweet spot. There's so much momentum in the air. It's the perfect time for spells that are meant to expand or blossom. The Full Moon feels like a spotlight. Everything brightens and intensifies. I often leave my jar spells out to soak up its light, especially if I need extra strength or clarity. This is where I proudly (not subtly) honor completions and celebrate progress.

As the moon begins to wane, you can try shifting gears. The energy turns inward. During the Waning Gibbous, lean into soft release, maybe for forgiveness work or a quiet goodbye. The Last Quarter will help you cut cords and let go of habits that keep you stuck. And by the Waning Crescent is great for when you're clearing the space for something new to grow.

Sometimes, I layer in the moon's zodiac sign too. If I'm making a money jar during a waxing moon in Taurus, I might use green herbs and coins to double down on stability and abundance. For a healing jar under a full moon in Cancer, it's all about emotional comfort—rose quartz, chamomile, maybe a tear or two I'm ready to shed.

Here's what I've found the New Moon is especially good for:

- ☽ Clearing out what no longer fits
- ☽ Starting something bold or fresh
- ☽ Doing deep shadow work
- ☽ Setting goals with real clarity

It's not just about when you cast a spell, it's about how the moon's energy shapes every part of it. It might influence the herbs you pick, the candle you light, or the word you carve into wax. For example, if I'm doing a protection jar, I'll go with black tourmaline and a black candle when the moon is waning to push energy away. But if I'm casting during the waxing phase, I might choose clear quartz and a white candle to strengthen my boundaries from within.

If the timing doesn't line up, that's okay. I've done plenty of spells outside the 'ideal' window. What matters most is awareness. If I know the moon is waning, I'll work with that energy, even if it's not what I originally planned. I often use a lunar journal to track how my spells feel and what works best for me. You might also want to start by keeping a simple moon calendar to mark out phases that align with the kind of work you want to do e.g., growth, release, protection, or healing. That way, you're not guessing. You're growing a relationship with the moon and letting that shape your practice in a natural, steady way. And remember, like me, you don't need to chase the 'perfect' phase. What matters is choosing the one that supports your intention, in your own rhythm and your own voice.

The changing seasons bring powerful energy shifts you can tap into with your jar spells. Each season has its own rhythm, and when you match your spells to that rhythm, you create stronger, more aligned magic.

Spring is all about growth and fresh starts, making it great for healing and renewal. Summer brings full, active energy, which is perfect for abundance or confidence spells. Autumn invites gratitude and helps you let go. Whereas Winter offers a quiet power for rest and rebirth.

Choose ingredients that echo the season. In spring, I like to use flower petals, fresh herbs, and green crystals. For summer, sun-dried rosemary, St. John's wort, and citrine work beautifully. Autumn spells love grains, nuts, and grounding stones. And in winter cloves and evergreens work best.

I used to think I had to follow old spell traditions to the letter. I'd panic if I didn't have the exact herb or if a sabbat slipped past without a ritual. It took me a while to realise those "rules" weren't fixed. They were patterns—things that worked for others at a certain time, in a certain place. Not commandments. More like whispers from the land, reminders to move with the season, not against it. So now, if I'm drawn to a summer herb in the middle of winter, I go with it. I don't need to explain why. The pull is reason enough. That's the magic: using what's around you, letting your intention do the heavy lifting.

Recently, we had a rare rainy, cool day in the middle of an unusually hot summer. A breeze came with the rain, carrying the scent of autumn. It felt like the perfect moment to create a spell for releasing anxiety and focusing on self-care — the kind of spell often saved for fall. Sometimes the Earth calls to you and your intentions, even when it isn't the traditional season.

Prosperity spells are a good example. I've cast them in every season, and they never come out the same. In spring, I'm all about fresh starts.

I reach for sprouting seeds, maybe some basil from the windowsill, anything that feels full of potential. Summer feels bold. That's when I speak louder, set clearer goals, bring in sun-warmed crystals or dried citrus. Autumn turns reflective. I think about what I've built and what I want to keep. There's a slowing down, a sense of gratitude. By winter, I go inward. I focus on quiet strength, on holding steady, on planting intentions I won't rush.

If I don't have what a spell "calls for", I don't stress. I use what I've got. Dried thyme can carry the same hope as spring blossoms, if that's what it means to me. No pine branches? A few drops of oil on cloth does the job. What matters is the meaning, not the match.

I don't always stick to the Wheel of the Year either. Sometimes the mood around me doesn't line up with the calendar. Instead, I notice the shift in the light, the smell of rain on warm soil, the way the wind changes. I keep a seasonal journal, nothing fancy—just scribbled notes about what I worked on and how it felt. Over time, I've found my own rhythm. That's what makes the magic stick. It's personal. Alive. Mine.

If you want to supercharge your seasonal jar spells, you can try using my cheat sheet to help you tap into each season's energy:

Spring (Renewal & Growth)

- Fresh herbs and sprouts
- Green or clear crystals
- Rainwater or morning dew
- Seeds and bulbs

Summer (Power & Manifestation)

- Sun-charged ingredients
- Bright flowers and herbs
- Golden or yellow stones
- Solar-infused water

Autumn (Transformation & Release)

- Dried leaves, grains, harvest herbs
- Earth-toned crystals
- Found objects from nature

Winter (Protection & Rebirth)

- Evergreens and winter berries
- Dark, grounding stones
- Snow or ice water

To start, cleanse your materials with the season's elements; think spring rain, summer sunlight, autumn smoke, or snow melt. As you build your jar, picture each ingredient carrying that seasonal charge straight into your spell. Seal with wax in a color that matches both your goal and the season (e.g., green for growth in spring, black for protection in winter), then activate it with fire, water, air, or earth—whatever feels right for the time of year. The more you tune in and sync your craft with nature's rhythms, the more your spells hum with power. You're working with the year, not apart from it.

There's more to timing than the moon. For extra strength, time your jar spells with planetary hours or power days, as these windows carry natural charge. Planetary hours split the day and night into twelve parts, each ruled by a different planet. These hours bring specific vibes you can tap into:

♀ Venus Hour – best for love, beauty, and harmony

♃ Jupiter Hour – great for money, luck, and growth

♂ Mars Hour – ideal for courage, protection, or cutting ties

☿ Mercury Hour – perfect for communication or travel spells

I used to think spell timing was something only ceremonial magicians cared about. But over time, I found that when I aligned my spells with the natural rhythm of the day, they felt sharper. More direct. I'm not saying you need a planetary chart pinned above your altar. But if you know the kind of energy each day carries, you can work with it, not against it.

This isn't about rules. It's about stacking the odds in your favor.

Each day has a particular feel:

- Sunday (Sun): confidence, visibility, power
- Monday (Moon): intuition, emotions, home
- Tuesday (Mars): courage, bold action, protection
- Wednesday (Mercury): ideas, communication, movement
- Thursday (Jupiter): money, growth, expansion
- Friday (Venus): love, beauty, pleasure
- Saturday (Saturn): structure, endings, boundary work

Say I'm making a prosperity jar. Thursday feels like the right day, especially during Jupiter's hour. For home protection, I might wait for a Monday night when the moon feels strong. Does it always line up? Of course not. Life gets messy. But when it does, I take advantage. Like me, you don't need to wait for the "perfect" time to cast a spell. You just need to know what kind of energy you're working with. That awareness makes the whole process feel more intentional. Like you're casting with the wind at your back instead of pushing uphill.

Some days carry an extra charge: solstices, equinoxes, cross-quarter days. They mark real shifts in the world around us. Many overlap with old festivals, which means you're tapping into something people have been doing for centuries. That kind of energy builds up over time. But it's important that you don't let the calendar boss you around. If you miss Venus hour on a Friday, you can still work with Venus energy the next time her hour comes around. What matters is knowing why you're choosing a certain time, and then making it work for you.

If you want to explore magical timing more deeply, here are a few things that help me:

- I check planetary hours based on where I live
- I note spell results in my journal, so I can see what timings worked
- I mark seasonal shifts and celestial events ahead of time
- I weave in bits of my natal chart if it feels right
- And I always stay flexible

Timing can help, but your magic lives in how you show up. You might add a few extras when you want things to click. For example, if I'm casting during Jupiter hour, I like to use herbs linked to Jupiter—like oak or sage—and choose colors like blue or purple. That way, the ingredients and timing echo each other. It creates this layered effect where everything points in the same direction. Still, I don't wait for the stars to align. If something needs doing, I get to it. Timing is a tool, not a leash. It's there to support your magic, not slow it down.

These days, with glowing screens and constant pings pulling us away from ourselves, it's no wonder we feel disconnected from the rhythms our ancestors knew so well. But they haven't disappeared. Those patterns of moonlight and shifting seasons are still moving and speaking to us. We must simply learn them from where we stand now.

Back then, people watched the moon rise and read the weather in the soil. Whereas we might check an app and get calendar alerts. Honestly, that works too. The energy doesn't care if you track it by sundial or smartphone. What matters is the connection.

If your life feels too full or unpredictable for anything big or ceremonial, here are a few things that help me stay grounded, which you might also find useful.

◊ Set a moon-charging spot on your windowsill. It doesn't need to be fancy. Just a ledge where you can place a glass of water, a crystal, or anything you want to soak up moonlight.

◊ Add gentle calendar reminders for things like moon phases or the solstice. That way, you don't miss the shift, especially when life feels rushed.

◊ Prep your jar spell ingredients ahead of time. Keep a small box or tin with herbs, paper scraps, or whatever you use most. That way, when the right moment shows up, you're ready.

◊ If all you get is ten quiet minutes in a day, claim them. Light a candle. Stir something with intention. Whisper a wish.

◊ Keep your altar simple. Even a tray with a few objects that matter—stones, photos, leaves from the garden—can hold just as much meaning as something elaborate. Let it shift with the seasons or your mood.

- ◊ Let go of the idea of "doing it right." Your prosperity jar might hold cinnamon and basil... and a folded business card. Your healing jar might cradle rose quartz and a printed prescription. That mix of old and new? That's magic. Real life magic.

You don't need perfect timing. You don't need rare herbs or the silence of midnight. You need intention. If all I have is my focus and a bit of moonlight through glass, that's enough.

Here's what's helped me keep spellwork simple and flexible. You might try one or two if life feels a little too full:

- ◊ Don't worry if you miss the exact moment of the full moon. Its energy lingers. Try working with it the day before or after. There's still magic in the window.
- ◊ Tune into the seasons by feel, not just by date. Watch the trees. Smell the rain. Let the shift in air or light guide you more than a calendar ever could.
- ◊ If you can't step outside, close your eyes and imagine the season you're working with. Call it in. Let it meet you where you are.
- ◊ Build rituals that fit the shape of your life. Forget what someone else says magic *should* look like. Start with what's real for you.
- ◊ And if it ever feels like you need more tools, more time, or more "rightness," remember this: our ancestors worked with what they had. So can we. That's where the power is.

That's the heart of it. Working with what's here. Staying open. Staying rooted. Letting the rhythm of the world meet you right where you are. You don't need incense or ceremonial robes. You can stir a cup of tea with intention. You can turn your windowsill into an altar. That's magic too. It's small things matter. Snapping photos of a seasonal shift. Writing a single line in a moon journal. Touching a leaf on the way to work. Sitting still with a plant for five minutes. These tiny choices will keep you connected.

Tapping into natural cycles is one of the most powerful and practical ways I've found to strengthen a jar spell. When your materials and intentions line up with the rhythm of the moon, seasons, or planetary hours, your magic naturally feels more effective, because you're working with the energy that's already flowing around you.

You can add extra power to your spells by layering these natural cycles. I usually start with the moon phase, then think about what season I'm in or what time of day it is. When those things match up, the energy really builds.

Here's how I make that work in real life:

- Each natural cycle supports certain types of magic.
- Stacking them—like casting a growth spell during a waxing moon in spring—adds strength.
- Your own energy matters too.
- And if the timing's not perfect? That's fine. Remember, intention matters more than perfection.

Start by picking the cycle that fits your goal. As I mentioned previously, I like to use the waxing moon for anything I want to grow, like confidence, love, or money. The waning moon helps me release things or create protection. And the full moon is my go-to for anything that needs a big boost or a clear ending. Then, consider the season. Spring feels like new beginnings, so try focusing on planting seeds and starting fresh. Summer is all about abundance. Autumn feels more reflective, good for closure and gratitude. While winter may draw you inward, which is a wonderful time for doing healing or protection work.

All of this can get specific if you want it to. Traditional guides might say, “Do a prosperity jar on a Thursday, during Jupiter’s hour, under a waxing moon.” And sure, that’s ideal. But if your life doesn’t line up that neatly, you can still create powerful results. I focus on intention first, then layer in ingredients or timing that support that energy, without stressing if the stars don’t all align.

Here are a few things that help me bring timing into my spellwork:

- Check what cycle you’re in, be that the moon phase, season, or time of day.
- Choose herbs and ingredients that match both your intention and the timing.
- Get your tools and space ready in advance when you can.
- Stay flexible. If something doesn’t line up, you can adapt.

Working with natural cycles isn’t about rules. It’s about paying attention to what’s already moving. When those layers line up, your jar spells flow. For example, a prosperity jar made during a waxing moon might include:

- Herbs gathered in spring, when growth energy is strong
- Crystals charged under a full moon
- A coin or charm that connects to Jupiter or abundance
- Something personal, like a written goal or a business card

It doesn’t have to be perfect. But when your choices reflect the energy of the cycle you’re working with, everything starts to click into place. And that’s when the magic really works.

As I said, keep a journal. Write down what works and what feels right, along with which combinations appear to hold the most power. Watch how the moon shifts your mood, and if certain spells land better in spring than in autumn. Over time, you'll fall into your own rhythm. Not a tight schedule, but something softer. Something that fits the way you actually live.

Magic has always worked with the world around it. You don't need still air or a full moon to cast a strong spell. What matters is your focus and intention. A modern life doesn't make old wisdom less powerful; it gives it new places to grow.

My friend, Emma, still tends her herb garden with real care. When she started, she tracked every moon phase. Each spell had a date, or a rule. It helped, for a while. But something shifted. She started to feel the work more than plan it. The light in the sky told her more than the calendar, and the plants themselves gave her cues. She stopped trying to follow every instruction and started listening instead. That's how you'll learn it too. Timing isn't about dates; It's about energy. The pull of a season. The stillness before change. Once you start noticing, you begin to feel part of something older. You sense the thread that runs through every spell and every hand that has worked this magic before you. As you follow that thread, your own practice takes root. It becomes something real, alive, and shaped by you.

CHAPTER 5

Building Spells That Hold Steady

Protective jar magic is old. Older than most things we practice now. People have been placing power in jars for thousands of years. You see it in Egyptian tombs, in Greek burial sites and in everyday folk traditions that passed down quietly through generations. Somewhere along the way, the purpose stayed the same, which was to guard, to hold, and to keep something safe. All of this still matters. You can make protective jars that calm a space or to support someone you love.

One friend of mine moved into a new house and felt tense from the start. The front door made her heart race. She and her partner kept bickering. Visitors left early. She'd read a bit about protective jars and decided to try one. She used what she had: black tourmaline, sea salt, rosemary from the garden. She charged the jar under the waning moon and buried it by the steps. Things shifted. The house felt different. Lighter. And the tension cleared. She added more jars at the four corners of the garden. For her, it wasn't about doing everything 'right', it was about paying attention, trusting herself, and taking quiet action. That made the space feel like home.

I'll walk you through how to choose a container, what to put inside, and how to sense when your spell is working. Whether you live in a single room or on open land, you can create protection that feels strong and alive.

This kind of magic doesn't come from fear. It comes from care. From wanting to feel steady, and from wanting the people and spaces you love to feel held. You're not copying the past. You're walking alongside it.

At the heart of protective jar magic is a simple idea: a jar isn't just a container. It holds your intention. It anchors the energy you're calling in and helps you shape strong, lasting boundaries.

This kind of spell usually draws strength from three key parts: the jar, the ingredients, and your focus. All of them matter, but not in equal measure. Some spells lean more on one than the others. That's fine.

The jar itself carries meaning. Clear glass helps the energy flow into your space. A dark bottle traps what you don't want escaping. Clay feels grounding. Metal brings a sharper charge. So before you begin, ask yourself how you want the spell to work. Then pick the jar that suits your purpose.

Now think about what you'll place inside. Each ingredient should have a job. I often use black tourmaline. It doesn't just block negativity—it helps shift it into something lighter. Rosemary acts like a shield. Sage clears out the leftovers. If you're missing those, plain salt works well. It's old magic. You'll find it in protection work all over the world.

As you build the jar, layer with care. Start with something heavy at the bottom. That could be salt or a small stone to anchor the energy. Then add herbs to move and stir the spell. Somewhere in the middle, place something that means something to you. A charm, a written name, a scrap of fabric. As you build, focus. You're not just filling a jar. You're crafting a boundary.

If you want to boost the energy, consider the timing. The waning moon supports protection and banishing. But don't wait if it doesn't feel right. If you need to act now, do it. The energy you bring will carry more weight than any calendar.

When the jar is full and sealed, it's time to activate it. That means giving it your energy. You could whisper words over it, pass it through smoke, place it on a windowsill at night, or hold it in your hands. Some people like to visualize. Others use Reiki. There's no right way, only the one that feels true.

Once it's working, keep a connection with it. You don't need to open it. A quick glance, a silent thank-you, or a short phrase spoken now and then is enough. Think of it like tending a fire. It doesn't take much, but it needs you to keep it alive.

These jars have lasted across generations because they work. They're more than decoration. They stand quietly, holding your energy, creating a barrier that protects you and the space around you.

Creating household protection wards using jar magic is one of the simplest and most effective ways to anchor protective energy. These jars act as quiet guardians. They help shield your home from negativity while encouraging peace and calm throughout your space. When placed with care, they can shift how your home feels on an energetic level.

A protection ward jar combines physical materials with a strong, clear intention. For general household protection, clear glass jars work well. They allow the energy to spread outward and make it easy to keep an eye on the jar over time. If a room feels heavy or especially vulnerable, use dark blue or black glass to help contain and neutralize unwanted energy. Choose the jar size based on what you're protecting. Small jars work for a single room, while larger ones suit the whole home.

Here's what you'll need for a basic household protection jar:

- A clean glass jar with a tight lid
- Black tourmaline or obsidian (or use black pebbles or sea salt as a substitute)
- Dried rosemary (or bay leaves or sage)
- Sea salt or kosher salt
- Protective herbs like lavender, sage, or cedar
- A white or black candle
- Protective oil (olive oil works well as a simple option)

Ideally, you'd create the jar during the waning moon. This phase is often used for banishing and protection. But if you need protection sooner, don't wait. Put extra focus into your process. A clear intention is more important than perfect timing.

To make your jar:

1. Cleanse all your materials using smoke, salt, or any method that feels right to you.
2. Begin with a layer of salt at the bottom to ground the energy.
3. Add your protective stones.

4. Place your herbs next, building them up around the stones.
5. Anoint the jar lid with oil in a clockwise motion while focusing on protection.
6. Seal the jar with melted candle wax.
7. Charge it by placing it in the moonlight or holding it in your hands while focusing your energy.

Once your jar is ready, decide where to place it. Think about how energy flows through your space. Common spots include the four corners of your home, near doors and windows, or anywhere that feels vulnerable. Some people like to place jars near Wi-Fi routers or electronic devices to act as a buffer.

Your jar will work best if you maintain a connection with it. You don't need to do anything elaborate. A daily moment of attention is enough. You might place a hand on the jar or say a quiet word of thanks. To recharge the energy, revisit your intention during the full moon or place the jar in moonlight for a few hours.

If you live in an apartment or can't place jars outside, make smaller versions. You can keep them on windowsills or tuck them near doors. The key is consistency—both in where you place them and how you interact with them.

Your own energy works alongside these jars. They don't replace personal awareness or other forms of spiritual protection. Instead, they support you. When combined with cleansing and regular attention, these jars become part of a wider protective system that nurtures both your space and your spirit.

Once you're confident with the basics, feel free to customize your jars. Think about what you're protecting and what kind of energy you want to welcome in. For example, placing citrine in a jar near your work area can help lift your mood and keep stress at bay. Personal touches like this make the magic feel more alive and more connected to your everyday life.

Creating a network of protective jars can be a powerful way to strengthen your energetic boundaries. Rather than relying on one jar, you create a system—several jars working together to form a protective field around your space. Each one carries its own energy while supporting the others. This idea echoes older traditions where people placed vessels at important points to anchor protection. You can shape it to suit your space. Think of it as weaving a fabric that holds and adjusts as your needs shift.

Start by choosing the area you want to protect. The simplest version uses four jars placed in the four directions. You can add more, especially if there are corners or spots in your space that feel open or heavy.

Inside each jar, you'll want:

- A base that grounds the spell, like sea salt, black tourmaline or obsidian
- Protective herbs that feel right for you
- A linking item to help tie the jars together. This could be a colored thread, a shared stone, or even a symbol

You can also add anything personal that reflects the kind of protection you're asking for. If the timing works, build your network during a waning moon. That said, I've built plenty of jar networks whenever the need arose. What matters is your focus as you prepare and place them.

To make a four-jar network, gather and cleanse all the jars at once. Keeping the ingredients consistent helps the energy stay stable, but you can also assign direction-based elements if that feels right. Place the jars in each corner of your space. I usually start in the North and move clockwise. As I set each one down, I picture a line of energy stretching to connect them.

Once your jars are in place, they'll need small acts of care. I check mine every month. A quick look to make sure they're whole. A moment of stillness to reconnect with their energy. I might adjust something if life has changed since I last tended them.

Later on, you might want to build more than one network. I've made an outer ring to block what doesn't belong, and a quieter one inside to protect focus and peace. Think of it as layers, each with its own job.

Repeating details across your jars helps keep the energy linked. You might tie them with the same thread or use the same symbol on each one. Even using the same type of stone can strengthen the connection.

You can bring this approach into digital spaces too. I've placed jars near devices to create a calmer energy while I work. If you live in a flat or share your space, you can still build a smaller network that fits your layout. The size doesn't matter. What matters is that the system makes sense to you.

If you're working with more than one network, it helps to give each one a clear job. You could vary the jar colors or ingredients to mark the difference. That way, the energy stays organized and you always know what's doing what.

The real strength of a jar network lies in how each part supports the whole. Together, they create a steady, adaptable field of protection. With time and care, this can become one of the most grounded forms of magic in your practice.

Looking after your protection jars is just as important as creating them. Think of them like a fire that needs tending or a garden that needs care. Without regular attention, their energy fades. Staying connected helps keep their strength steady.

These jars work by absorbing negative energy. Over time, that takes a toll. Checking in on them helps you stay ahead of that slow drain and gives you a chance to adjust your boundaries when life shifts.

You might notice when a jar needs refreshing. Your space could feel unsettled, or the energy around the jar might seem dull or off. Herbs may lose their color. Wax might crack. Liquids can turn cloudy. When that happens, the jar has likely done its job and needs renewal.

To care for it, start by cleansing the outside. Smoke or saltwater works well. Recharge the jar when the moon is waning or simply when it feels like the right time. Set your intention clearly. If the wax seal has cracked, add a fresh layer. If the contents feel faded, top them up. As you do, pause for a breath or a quiet word of thanks. That moment of connection helps anchor the work.

You don't need fancy tools. If you only have table salt, use that. Hold it for a moment and focus. If moonlight isn't available, visualize the light instead. What matters most is showing up with clear purpose.

When you're looking after a network of jars, the care takes a bit more time. A steady rhythm helps. Start with the first jar you made and move through the others one by one. Picture the connection between them as you go. If you can, refresh them all within the same moon cycle. Update the ingredients if your needs or space have shifted.

Some people prefer to create new jars every six months. Others use the same ones for much longer. Either way, what matters is staying in tune with how each jar feels.

When a jar feels finished, it's time to release it. Start by thanking it for the protection it gave. If the timing works, take it apart during the waning moon. Return natural elements to the earth, away from the space you're guarding. Cleanse the jar if you want to reuse it or dispose of it with intention.

As time goes on, your connection with each jar grows. This kind of regular care isn't about keeping the spell active. It deepens your awareness of what you're holding, what you're guarding, and how you move through the world. Your jars become more than objects. They become quiet, steady companions in your practice.

Protective jar magic has changed over time. These days, many people combine old methods with new materials to create jars that honor ancestral practices while fitting into modern life. This approach keeps traditions alive and helps you protect your space in a way that works for you.

In the 16th and 17th centuries, people in England and North America used "witch bottles" to guard against harm. These jars were filled with pins, nails, herbs, and personal items, then buried upside down near the home as a long-lasting shield. You can draw on this history and adapt it to your own needs and beliefs.

When working with both old and new tools, it helps to understand the role each one plays. Pins and nails can break up or trap harmful energy. Crystals like black tourmaline offer a gentler way to achieve a similar result. You can use both to build a layered, powerful spell.

Here's one way to create a protection jar using a mix of traditional and modern tools:

- Start with a base of black salt and crystal chips to absorb and strengthen.
- Add herbs such as basil or angelica, and a few drops of essential oil.

- Include something sharp like a pin or needle, along with a written affirmation or sigil.
- Seal the jar with wax. Add resin if you want a long-lasting finish.

Make sure your ingredients work together. In the past, people might have added blood or urine to link the jar to themselves. Today, you can use a strand of hair, a nail clipping, or a small personal item. You might also include something more modern, like a crystal grid or a piece of tech, especially if you want to block digital interference. Choose what feels right to you.

You can align your spell with moon phases or planetary hours, but don't let timing stop you. The most important part is your intention and the care you bring to the process. If you're missing certain ingredients, you can still make something powerful. Table salt is fine if you charge it with purpose. Herbs from your garden are just as useful as ones bought from a shop. What matters is how you use them, not how rare or fancy they are.

When building a blended protection jar:

- Cleanse each item beforehand in a way that feels meaningful to you.
- Place the ingredients mindfully and with clear purpose.
- Choose a sealing method that suits your style. Wax, thread, and resin all work well.
- Activate the jar in a way that connects with you. This might involve speaking your intent, holding quiet focus, or doing a brief energy practice.

To keep the jar working, check in with it regularly. You don't need to open it—just cleanse the outside now and then or revisit your intention. Your ongoing connection is what keeps it strong and responsive.

Blending old and new tools can add depth to your practice. Protection jars don't need to follow a single tradition. They gain power when they reflect both your history and your present needs. A single jar by your door can shift the energy in your home. A full network can deepen and extend that effect.

The most important thing is clarity. A jar is more than herbs or stones. It holds your intent. It helps define your boundary. It supports the kind of space you want to live in.

Protection Enhancements With Different Salt Types

- **Salt- Rock, table** - All-purpose Protection, Absorbing Negative Energy Cleansing
- **Pink Salt** – Love, Stability, Security
- **Black Salt** - Banishing, Boundaries, Curses, Hexes, Removes Negative Energy, Break Hexes and Reverse Magic
- **Grey Salt** – Grounding, Balancing, Cleansing, Protection
- **Red Salt** – Attraction, Love, Passion, Strengthen Willpower and Courage

CHAPTER 6

A Pinch of Basil, a Bit of Hope

Generations of practitioners passed down the gentle craft of healing and prosperity jars, understanding that wellbeing and abundance are deeply connected. Like a garden, these jars take time and care. They create space for healing to unfold and growth to take root, offering support for your body, emotions, and daily life.

Healers have long known that real prosperity isn't about money. It includes good health, emotional steadiness, and a sense of meaning. When you make jars that invite both healing and abundance, you align with this older way of thinking. The results tend to feel steadier and more lasting.

In my own work, I've noticed how easily these two energies weave together. Chamomile is a good example. It's gentle and calming, yet it's also known to draw in luck. Adding it to a jar brings both comfort and momentum in a single, quiet spell.

A friend of mine, Sheila, once saw health and money as separate challenges. One winter, both started slipping. Her energy dropped, and so did her income. In a moment of quiet resolve, she made a jar that spoke to both needs. She used a mason jar, added rose quartz for care, green aventurine for fresh openings, chamomile to ease her nerves, and cinnamon to call in flow.

As she built the jar, she noticed something. Without health, it's hard to chase opportunity. Without a stable base, healing doesn't stick. Each day she spent a few minutes with the jar, holding it, breathing with it, imagining light filling her space. Nothing changed overnight. But sleep came easier. Work felt less draining. Small chances turned into real steps forward. Six months on, she landed a promotion—not from one lucky moment, but because her energy was more focused, her body stronger, her mindset clearer.

This chapter will guide you through making jars that support both healing and prosperity. You'll learn how to choose ingredients that feel right, how to build each layer with care, and how to tend to your jars over time. Whether you're focused on physical renewal, opening new paths, or strengthening the bond between the two, this practice can help you grow the kind of support that lasts.

Practitioners have always grounded healing and prosperity magic in the idea that health and abundance support one another. When your body feels steady, it's easier to pursue what you want. When you feel secure, wellbeing follows more naturally. This balance is what makes certain spell jars feel so effective.

Rather than separating healing from prosperity, this kind of magic brings the two together. It draws from energies like growth, renewal, and expansion. Many older practitioners used overlapping herbs and crystals for both purposes, trusting in the deep connection between feeling well and living well.

To build stronger jars, focus on a few simple foundations:

Intention

Get clear on what you want. Are you calling in physical healing, a financial shift, or something that blends both?

Correspondence

Choose herbs, stones, and colors that speak to your goal and feel aligned with your energy.

Timing

Work with natural rhythms. A waxing moon supports growth, and spring brings renewal. These patterns help carry your spell further.

When your magic is rooted in clarity and balance, the results feel more whole. It helps your outer actions and inner state move in the same direction.

Choosing your ingredients matters—not just because of what they stand for but because of the energy they bring into your space. Practitioners have always grounded healing and prosperity magic in the idea that health and abundance support one another.

If your focus is on healing, try working with:

Chamomile

Gentle and grounding, it calms the body and invites rest. A quiet but steady presence in any healing jar.

Rose quartz

A crystal of care. It helps you soften toward yourself, which is often where true healing begins.

For prosperity spells, reach for:

Cinnamon

Warming and sharp, it stirs things up and helps move stuck energy.

Green aventurine

Known for opening the way. It offers gentle encouragement for growth and fresh opportunity.

When to work

Moon cycles can offer structure if you're looking to time your spell:

- A waxing moon helps you call things in.
- A full moon gives extra power to your focus.
- A waning moon helps you release blocks and let go of what's weighing you down.
- A new moon invites fresh starts and quiet intention setting.

With the right timing and ingredients, your jar becomes more than symbolic. It turns into a living, working part of your practice.

Small choices, quiet power

Your jar isn't just a vessel. It plays a part in how the energy flows. Color, shape, and timing all bring something to the spell.

- Transparent glass keeps your intention visible. It's great if you want to stay connected visually.
- Blue jars carry a healing, calming tone.
- Green jars support growth, security, and financial steadiness.
- Round jars keep energy moving gently.

- Square jars offer a firmer base, good for structure and grounding.

You can also choose your time of day based on what you're calling in:

- Morning carries fresh energy and a sense of hope.
- Midday feels strong and assertive, good for action and calling in success.
- Evening supports deep healing and longer-term shifts.

A quiet reminder

Healing and prosperity magic become more powerful when you let them support each other. Feeling well makes it easier to receive abundance. Having enough makes it easier to rest and recover. That's the root of this practice: honoring the link between being well and living well.

A jar spell becomes something deeper when it reflects this balance. It's not just a collection of ingredients. It's a way to steady your own rhythm and invite in a life that holds both care and growth. You're not just following a tradition. You're letting it meet your present moment.

Crafting a wellness jar doesn't need to be complex or depend on rare ingredients. What matters most is the intention behind your work and an understanding of what each element brings to the spell.

Herbs

Herbs often form the heart of a wellness jar. They carry gentle, steady healing energy.

◊ Chamomile supports rest and emotional ease. If you don't have any on hand, mint or lemon balm make calming, accessible alternatives.

- ◊ Lavender is well known for its relaxing qualities and can also bring clarity. Rosemary adds a purifying edge and can stand in for lavender when needed.

Crystals

Modern practitioners often add crystals to jar magic to focus intention and provide energetic support.

- ◊ Amber connects to warmth and vitality. It's deeply rooted in healing traditions.
- ◊ Clear quartz acts as a magnifier and helps energize whatever else is in the jar.
- ◊ Bloodstone encourages courage and physical resilience. If it's unavailable, red jasper offers a similarly grounding energy and may be easier to find.
- ◊ Simple crystals work just as well as expensive ones. It's the energy you bring to the work that activates their potential.

Salt

Many cultures have used salt in magical practices for its direct and protective energy.

- ◊ Pink salt supports gentle purification. Black salt is often used to banish heavy or lingering energy.If you're using plain table salt, that works too—just hold it in your hands for a moment and focus your intent. The strength comes from the way you use it.

Affirmations

A short written affirmation adds direction to your jar. It gives shape to your energy and offers something to return to when you need to refocus.

- ◊ Try something simple like:
  I welcome calm and healing.

◊ Slip the paper inside your jar and let it act as a personal anchor.

Essential Oils

Essential oils offer a concentrated form of plant energy. A single drop is often enough.

◊ Lavender oil can stand in for dried lavender.

◊ Citrus oils lift the mood and clear out stuck or heavy feelings. Start small—one or two drops is plenty for a wellness jar.

Choosing Your Ingredients

While traditional associations are helpful, don't ignore your personal bond with an ingredient. A spell might call for comfrey, but if you feel more connected to calendula growing in your garden, that connection can carry more weight. Use the plants, stones, and symbols that feel right to you.

Clarity in your purpose and trust in your materials go further than strict rules ever will.

Timing

Working with natural rhythms adds another layer to your spell. The waxing moon supports energy and growth. Spring is a time of new beginnings and gentle return.

But if the moment calls for it, don't wait. A strong, present intention can move energy even when the timing isn't traditional.

A Simple Wellness Jar

Try this gentle combination to begin:

◊ A small handful of chamomile or lemon balm

◊ Clear quartz or rose quartz for emotional support

◊ A pinch of salt to clear and protect

◊ A written affirmation focused on healing

◊ Three drops of lavender oil

Layer everything slowly into a clean glass jar. As you add each item, pause and feel its energy. When you're ready, seal the jar with white or blue wax—both are linked with peace and renewal.

Keep it somewhere you'll see it often. Your nightstand, altar, or a quiet corner all work well. A jar works best when you stay connected to it.

Expanding Your Practice

If you'd like to go further, create a central wellness jar and place smaller jars around it—one for emotional clarity, one for physical support, another for spiritual grounding. This approach creates a gentle ecosystem of care, tailored to your specific needs.

The most effective wellness jars are often the most personal. When your materials feel meaningful, your spell holds more weight. It's okay to shift, substitute, or change things as you go. What matters is that your choices feel honest and aligned with the life you're trying to build.

I've found that working with prosperity magic comes with real responsibility. It's not just about drawing in wealth. It's about doing so with care—honoring the energies you're calling on and thinking about how your abundance fits into the wider world.

What's always stayed with me is this: real prosperity isn't about taking more, but about flowing with what's already present. When I build a jar spell, I try to listen to what feels right. The ingredients become part of a language—one that speaks not just to my desires, but to my values too.

Cinnamon is often my starting point. Its warmth wakes things up. I've used it many times to help get things moving—whether I'm feeling stuck in work or need to call in fresh energy. A pinch from the spice rack works just as well as anything fancy. The power is in how I use it.

Basil has a special place in my practice. I learned early on that it's long been used for prosperity, and it always feels like a steadying presence. When I grow it myself, I like to use the fresh leaves. But I've also opened my cupboard and reached for dried basil when that's what I had. It still works. What matters is the intention I set as I place it in the jar.

I don't always use crystals, but when I do, I'm drawn to green aventurine or citrine for their associations with opportunity and movement. Still, I know that not everyone has access to them—and I've had moments where I didn't either. In those times, I've picked up a small green pebble from the garden or used clear quartz I already had. If I speak my intention clearly, those stones hold the same weight.

Color plays a quiet but powerful role too. I often wrap jars in green or gold ribbon or melt wax in those colors to seal them. They remind me of what I'm calling in—growth, clarity, and enough. And while I often work during the waxing moon, I don't wait around for perfect timing. If something's needed, I begin. Intention has always carried me further than timing alone.

Before I do any abundance work, I pause and ask myself: *Why do I want this?* Am I seeking something that will support not just me, but the people around me too? Real prosperity, I've learned, includes joy, wellness, and the chance to give as much as we receive.

Here's one of the first prosperity jars I made with this in mind:

- A base of cinnamon for momentum
- Three basil leaves for steady growth
- A green pebble I found while walking
- A bay leaf with my intention written on it
- Green thread to bind it all together

As I placed each item in the jar, I spoke aloud:

May this abundance come in ways that bring no harm. May it nourish not only my life, but the lives I touch.

Reciprocity is part of my practice too. I often follow spells like these with action—donating to a cause, helping a friend, or sharing resources. It reminds me that magic isn't just personal; it's relational.

I've also played with timing. Dawn often feels like a good moment to invite fresh opportunity, while midday holds a strong, focused energy that works well when I want quick results.

Over time, I began creating networks of jars, each with a different focus. One for steady income. One for career shifts. One to support the financial wellbeing of my family. Linking them through shared herbs or colors helped them feel connected—like parts of the same conversation.

These jars aren't one-and-done spells. I come back to them. I recharge them. I rewrite the intentions as things evolve. Through this, I've learned that prosperity magic isn't about chasing wealth. It's about staying in right relationship with what I need, what I offer, and the energy I move through the world. And that's what keeps it working.

One of the most powerful shifts I made in my magical practice was learning to combine healing and prosperity within a single jar. It might sound simple, but the impact runs deep. When you bring these two energies together—wellbeing and abundance—you open the door to real, lasting transformation. It's a reminder that health supports prosperity, and prosperity helps us rest, heal, and grow.

I learned early on that certain ingredients naturally support both. Take **mint**, for example. It's known for clearing the mind and body, but it also draws in business luck. That's the kind of overlap I look for when building a combination jar—something that speaks to both the body and the bank account.

If you're creating your first healing-and-prosperity jar, here are a few ingredients I've worked with and trust:

- **Green Aventurine**: A gentle ally for the heart. It invites in healing and opportunity.
- **Amethyst**: Helps with emotional release and attracts spiritual wealth.
- **Mint**: Clears out stagnant energy and supports success.
- **Thyme**: Strengthens the body while quietly drawing wealth.
- **Basil**: Balances emotions and supports sustainable abundance.
- **Cinnamon**: Sparks momentum in both healing and money matters.

I usually align this kind of work with the waxing moon when energy builds and expands. But I've also done it during the new moon, especially when I'm setting fresh intentions. If I'm clearing out blocks to either health or abundance, I'll use the waning moon.

When I build my jar, I start with **salt** for grounding. Then I layer in my chosen crystals, herbs, and a few drops of oil if it feels right. I let my intuition guide the order. Sometimes I hold each ingredient in my hand and ask, *how are you going to help me?*

Writing a clear petition helps bring it all together. I've used something like:

"As I grow stronger and healthier, abundance flows with ease. As I receive support and resources, I feel more grounded and whole." You might write your own or speak it aloud as you work. There's no right or wrong—only what feels honest and aligned.

If you want to take it further, you can create a set of connected jars. I've done this myself—a main jar for overall wellbeing, and smaller ones focused on things like career growth, emotional balance, or physical energy. I use shared ingredients to link them, like they're speaking to each other.

The more I've worked with these combination jars, the more I've realized that following someone else's list of ingredients will only get you so far. What really matters is your relationship to the elements. How does basil feel in your hands? What does aventurine mean to you? That kind of attention shapes your magic far more than any how-to guide.

To keep your jar working, you'll need to check in with it. I do this on the full moon for power, and the new moon for fresh direction. I might add a drop of oil, relight a candle near it, or just sit with it and breathe, picturing healing and abundance flowing together.

As you deepen your practice, keep in mind that true prosperity should never come at the cost of your wellbeing—and healing should leave room for comfort, security, and joy. When these energies are in balance, they reinforce each other. They ripple out into your life and the lives around you. This kind of jar isn't about magic. It's about learning to support your whole self. When you bring healing and prosperity into the same space, you create something steady, nourishing, and real. Something that grows with you.

I used to think timing in magic was all about the moon, until I realized it's about rhythm. The way the earth breathes, the moon waxes and wanes, the seasons shift. These rhythms hold power. When I started paying attention, my spell jars didn't just feel more effective—they felt more alive.

You don't need to memorize a lengthy list of correspondences to make the timing work for you. What matters is noticing what's happening around you and within you. If the air feels full of new beginnings, that might be your time to act. If everything feels like it's slowing down or falling away, that might be your moment to let go.

The moon is the easiest place to start. I always think of the new moon as a blank page. It's when I plant seeds—ideas, intentions, hope. Healing jars I make now are gentle ones, focusing on rest and recovery. Prosperity jars might aim for new income streams or fresh starts. There's something soft and full of promise about this phase.

As the moon waxes, that energy builds. I find this a good time to do the work—especially anything related to growth. Jars made now often focus on strengthening something already in motion, whether it's confidence, health, or money flow.

By the full moon, everything feels louder. It's a peak, and I use that power to charge what I've already made. If I've been working on a spell jar, this is when I'll speak my intention out loud or light a candle beside it. Sometimes, I'll make a jar from scratch now—but usually only if I really need a boost.

When the moon wanes, I focus on letting go. I've crafted jars to release worry, clear stuck energy, or shift limiting beliefs about money or worth. If you've been feeling heavy, this might be your moment to lighten the load.

Just before the new moon, we enter the dark moon. This is where deep change happens. I don't always work during this time, but when I do, it's usually big. Transformation jars, shadow work, or anything that asks me to go inward.

And then there are the seasons. I don't follow them perfectly, but I do notice the difference.

In spring, I lean into growth. It's a good time for jars that support new habits or beginnings.

Summer feels bold and abundant. If I'm working on money, visibility, or confidence, I like to use this energy.

In autumn, I focus on harvest and grounding. I'll make jars to stabilize income or protect my energy.

Winter pulls me inward. Healing jars feel more potent then, especially ones aimed at long-term change.

Sometimes, I combine both lunar and seasonal timing. A prosperity jar made during the waxing moon in spring always feels powerful to me—it's like double growth energy. But honestly? You don't need the perfect moment. I made some of my most important jars during messy, urgent times—not under ideal moon phases.

What helped me most was keeping a little magical calendar. I didn't make it complicated—just moon phases, seasonal shifts, and a few notes on how I was feeling. It helped me notice patterns and plan without losing the magic.

Here are a few ways I work with timing now:

- Charging jars under moonlight—full moon for power, new moon for fresh starts
- Crafting during equinoxes or solstices to match the season's mood
- Working with the time of day—dawn for beginnings, noon for strength, dusk for release
- Sometimes I check planetary hours, but only when it feels relevant

There are also times when I need to act now. If you're in a moment of need, you can still make your jar. You might acknowledge the current phase—maybe you're letting go of lack before inviting in wealth. Or maybe you're using the tail end of winter to set intentions for future growth. The important thing is that it feels right to you.

As you keep going, you might start building networks of jars that each hold a piece of your intention. I've made healing sets before—one jar to begin the process, another to build strength, a third to empower the whole system, and a final one to release what's no longer needed.

The best time to make a jar is when you feel called to. Timing helps—but it doesn't override your intuition. And remember, healing and prosperity don't live in separate corners. When you feel safe and nourished, it's easier to heal. When your body feels good, abundance has space to land. I've seen how a single ingredient, like green aventurine or chamomile, can support both. And I've learned that small actions, repeated with care, are often what create lasting change. So if you're starting now, keep it simple. Stay open. Let your jars reflect who you are and where you are. The cycles of nature aren't rules—they're companions.

CHAPTER 7

Building Spells from Scratch (and Hope)

The most powerful spells I've made didn't come from a book. They came from a feeling, a moment, or a sudden knowing that flickered through me like a match strike. You'll reach a point, too, where the recipes aren't enough. Where you start asking: what would happen if I made this mine? That's where the magic deepens.

A friend of mine stood barefoot in her garden once, twilight soft around her, gathering herbs for a spell she hadn't read in any book. She'd always followed traditional jars before. This time was different. Her best friend was dreading a big presentation and tied up with anxiety. None of the usual spells felt right, so she trusted the pull and followed it. She picked lavender for calm, rosemary for focus, a chip of blue kyanite she'd carried before her own speech, and a pinch of coffee grounds (because her friend swore by her morning brew). It worked. Her friend felt grounded and clear, like someone had steadied her hand.

I've never forgotten that. It reminded me that spellwork isn't about throwing ingredients into a jar and hoping for the best. It's about knowing why each one's there. Trusting your own sense of what fits. That's how you start to craft your own magic. This doesn't mean throwing tradition out the window. Far from it. Think of it more like learning to speak a language. You begin by repeating what others say. Then slowly, you start stringing together your own thoughts. The same goes for spell jars. You borrow, adapt, and eventually, you speak with your own voice.

Every jar spell I make rests on three things: correspondence, intent and energy. When you align those three things, something clicks. The spell feels grounded. Real. Personal.

Let's start with correspondence. Think of it as the language of magical ingredients—the bridge between the physical and the energetic. Rosemary doesn't protect just because a book told you so. It protects because it clears space, sets firm boundaries, and has centuries of use in healing and preservation. When you understand the why behind an ingredient, you can work more intuitively. You might reach for cayenne when you want something fiery and strong or use a soft piece of pink sea glass in place of rose quartz—especially if it already holds meaning for you.

When I'm making a protection jar, here are a few things I often include:

- Black tourmaline to ground the energy
- Sea salt to purify

- Rosemary to cleanse and reset
- Black wax to absorb what I want to release

But your choices might be different. That's part of the magic.

Once you've chosen your ingredients, get clear on your intention. This is your direction. Stay focused rather than aiming for direction. Vague wishes tend to scatter. Instead of thinking, "I just want to feel safe," try something like, "I create space where I feel protected, calm, and in control." The more specific and heart-led your words, the more power they carry.

Here's what helps make an intention strong:

- A clear purpose
- Words that speak to what you want, not just what you fear
- A grounding in your personal values
- A connection that feels real and meaningful to you

Next comes energy—the spark that brings it all to life. Some of that comes from nature: the pull of the moon, the shift in seasons, even the time of day. The rest? That's yours. It builds when you lay out your ingredients, stir the herbs, speak the words, and seal the jar. You don't need to be theatrical. Sometimes the quietest moments hold the most power.

These three threads—correspondence, intention, energy—they're not separate. They loop and feed into each other. Your intention shapes your ingredient choices. Your ingredients influence the kind of energy you raise. That energy circles back into your intention. When everything aligns, your spell starts to hum. It feels alive.

When I make a new jar, I usually:

- Take time to feel into what I want to shift or support
- Choose ingredients that match that energy—whether that's based on tradition, gut instinct, or memory
- Decide how I'll raise energy (sometimes through breath, sometimes timing, sometimes music or movement)
- Write it all down—not because I need to repeat it exactly, but because I want to learn from it

You don't have to abandon tradition to work this way. If anything, learning the roots helps you make meaningful choices. Like a good cook who understands flavor before riffing on a recipe, you'll learn how to make each spell your own.

As you keep going, you'll notice patterns. Certain herbs might always feel right to you. Some phases of the moon might amplify your work. Maybe you find that jars sealed with thread feel more potent than ones sealed with wax. Trust those patterns—they're the beginnings of your magical voice. Something grounded. Something evolving. Something only you can create.

Colors and Their Magical Properties

- **Red** – Fire, Passion, Courage, Assertiveness
- **Orange** – Creativity, Abundance, Confidence, Positivity
- **Yellow** – Happiness, Friendship, Inspiration, Learning, Knowledge, Business
- **Green** – Fertility, Change, Abundance, Luck, Healing, Peace & Prosperity, Money

- **Blue** – Water, Relaxation, Loyalty, Peacefulness, Inspiration, Trust
- **Purple** – Spirituality, Power, Magic, Enlightenment, Wisdom, Imagination
- **Pink** – Acceptance, Beauty, Compassion, Self-love, Nurturing, Kindness, Affection
- **Brown** – Endurance, Stability, Balance, Security, Harmony

Creating your own symbol system is a natural next step in your magical practice. You can think of it like learning a new visual language. It helps you express your intentions in a way that feels deeply personal. At its heart, this is a form of sympathetic magic: like attracts like. But instead of relying only on traditional signs, you're tuning into your own energy and intuition.

Symbols function as a bridge between what you want and the energy you're working with. While signs like spirals, hearts, or pentagrams carry long histories, the most powerful symbols are often the ones that come from your own experience. They mean something to you, which makes your magic stronger.

To start building your own set, pay attention to what naturally draws you in. You might find inspiration in:

- Patterns in nature
- Simple geometric shapes
- Dreams or flashes of imagery
- Cultural or ancestral roots
- Random marks you doodle without thinking

Choose the symbols that feel charged—not just visually, but emotionally or energetically. They don't need to be complex. Some of the most effective symbols are just a few lines or shapes that feel right when you look at them.

Once you have a few, start using them in your jar spells. You could:

- Draw one on the jar, lid, or label
- Add it to a note inside the jar
- Include it during an important part of your ritual, like when you seal or charge the jar

Keep track of what you try and how it feels. Over time, you'll start to notice patterns. Some symbols may feel especially useful for clarity, protection, or healing. As you keep working, your symbol system will grow with you.

Here are a few tips to guide your process:

- Decide where to place each symbol—on the outside, on a tag, or inside the jar
- Choose when to add them—during preparation, charging, or sealing
- Mix personal and traditional symbols if you like how they work together
- Try using assorted colors or materials like ink, wax, or thread

Let your system shift as you do. What speaks to you now may change as your practice deepens. That's a good thing. A personal symbol system is meant to evolve over time. You can also layer symbols with ingredients you already love. If you're using rose quartz for love, for example, try adding a symbol that feels like heart healing to you. When these elements come together, your jar becomes more than a spell. It becomes a reflection of your own energy and intention.

These symbols won't replace the foundations of spellwork. But they can support and deepen your practice. When you use them with care and purpose, they help you focus, bring more clarity, and connect with the work in a way that's truly your own.

When you're testing new spell combinations, you need both structure and instinct. I think of it like any creative practice. It deepens when you slow down, pay attention, and adjust based on what actually shows up. You don't need to get it perfect. You just need to stay curious and grounded. One of the biggest shifts for me came when I got specific. Instead of writing vague goals like "bring good luck," I'd say, "I want three new job leads this month" or "I want to feel calmer at home." When you're that clear, it's easier to notice what's working.

If you're in the thick of testing things, here's what's helped me:

- Keep a journal. Track everything—ingredients, timing, the moon phase, the weather, what was going on for you that day, and what happened afterward.
- Change one thing at a time. If you swap out an herb, keep the rest the same. That way, you know what's making the difference.
- Try making a control jar with neutral ingredients to compare.
- Give it time—at least one full moon cycle—to show results.
- Use divination (tarot, runes, whatever you work with) before and after to feel into what's moving beneath the surface.

Your journal becomes more than a notebook. It's a mirror for your magic. Over time, you'll spot patterns. For example, herbs that always support you, timings that feel stronger, phrases that carry real charge. This is how you build your own rhythm. For me, checking in with tarot before I seal the jar—and again once it's been sitting—gives me insight I'd otherwise miss. You might find your own way to sense those shifts too.

And then there's the practical stuff:

- Use safe, non-toxic ingredients and label everything clearly.
- Seal your jars tightly
- Keep them away from kids and pets.
- Write everything down—you'll be glad you did.

Sometimes it helps to invite another set of eyes. A trusted friend might spot something you missed or confirm a gut feeling you've been sitting with. Try repeating the same spell under a different moon phase or season. See what changes. You don't have to start from scratch every time. Instead, adjust as you go along. If something feels off, look at the timing, the words, the energy you were in. A small shift might be all it takes.

When you test spells this way, you build something solid. You stop second-guessing. You create a toolkit that works—not because someone else said so, but because it's yours. Lived, tested, real.

Common Crystals and their Primary Energy

Grounding

1. **Hematite** – Strong Earth connection, stabilizing.
2. **Smoky Quartz** – Absorbs negativity, anchors energy.
3. **Black Tourmaline** – Protective and grounding.
4. **Red Jasper** – Nurturing, promotes endurance.
5. **Obsidian** – Deep grounding and truth-revealing.

Protection

1. **Black Tourmaline** – Shields from harmful energy.
2. **Obsidian (Black)** – Psychic protection and grounding.
3. **Labradorite** – Deflects unwanted energies.
4. **Amethyst** – Spiritual protection, transmutation.
5. **Onyx** – Strengthens inner resolve and boundaries.

Love

1. **Rose Quartz** – Universal love, compassion.
2. **Rhodonite** – Emotional healing, forgiveness.
3. **Pink Kunzite** – Heart-opening and gentle love.
4. **Emerald** – Loyalty, deep romantic connection.
5. **Morganite** – Unconditional love, soul partnerships.

Luck

1. **Green Aventurine** – "Stone of opportunity."
2. **Citrine** – Attracts abundance and optimism.
3. **Jade (Green)** – Prosperity and good fortune.
4. **Tiger's Eye** – Confidence and favorable outcomes.
5. **Pyrite** – Success and lucky opportunities.

Prosperity

1. **Citrine** – Wealth and abundance magnet.
2. **Pyrite** – Manifestation of financial success.
3. **Green Aventurine** – Opportunity and growth.
4. **Malachite** – Transformation and prosperity flow.
5. **Peridot** – Attracts wealth and well-being.

Innovation is part of magic. But it only holds power when it's rooted in ethics. When you create new jar spells, you carry a responsibility—not just to yourself, but to others, to your community, and to the traditions you draw from.

Before casting, don't stop at asking, "What do I want?" Ask, "What could this affect?" That shift in thinking is where ethical practice begins. It's about honesty with yourself and a willingness to look at consequences.

Here are a few principles I come back to again and again:

- Always respect consent and autonomy
- Avoid doing harm—even if unintentional

- Honor the origins of cultural practices
- Choose materials that don't deplete the earth
- Stay accountable to the people around you

Consent really does matter. When you aim a spell at someone else, even if you mean well, it can cross a line fast. Supporting someone is not the same as trying to steer their choices. You'll feel the difference if you pause and check your intent.

Cultural respect matters too. If you're working with something from a tradition that isn't your own, take the time to learn about it properly. Ask where it comes from, who holds it, and whether you have the right to use it. If you do include it, name it. Give credit. Don't rewrite someone else's practice as your own.

Then there's the land itself. Some magical ingredients are overharvested, endangered, or pulled from places already under strain. When you can, use local plants or more sustainable options that still carry the energy you need. Magic can adapt—it always has.

I keep a record of every new spell I try. Not just what I used and what happened, but why I made it, and what I was hoping to shift. Writing it down keeps me honest. It also helps when I want to share something, because I can mark what comes from tradition and what I've made my own.

Here are a few practices that have helped me stay grounded in my craft:

- Do your research before trying something new
- Track what happens—including any side effects
- Ask trusted peers for feedback
- Own the impact of your spell, whether it helped or caused harm
- Be open to critique. Stay willing to change

If something feels ethically messy and you can't tell why, talk it through with someone you trust. Sometimes we miss our own blind spots. Another set of eyes can bring clarity. At the heart of it, ethical magic is about balance. It's learning how to stay creative while still being respectful. It's about building your own path without forgetting the ones that came before you. Your work will become part of something bigger. So make it something others can learn from. Let it carry strength, care, and the kind of integrity that lasts.

A good idea is only the beginning. To turn it into a reliable spell, you need more than inspiration. You need a record. Something clear and honest that shows what worked, what didn't, and what you might do differently next time.

Early alchemists wrote everything down. And that's what you'll be doing, learning through experience and building something that lasts.

Why it's always good to keep notes:

- To learn and repeat the spells that worked
- To spot what strengthens or weakens a result
- To build a grimoire that reflects what you've learned

What to include:

- A clear name for the spell and its purpose
- The date, moon phase and timing
- Every ingredient and how much you used

- What you did to prepare and activate it
- What you noticed while casting
- What happened afterward
- Any changes you'd make next time

Use a journal or notebook that suits you. It doesn't need to be fancy. Just organized enough that you can find what you need later, and open enough to include thoughts and feelings as they come up.

Once a spell is cast, I give it space—and then I watch. I write down anything that stands out, from big shifts to subtle mood changes. Then I start adjusting, step by step.

Here's what I tend to review:

- What I used and how much
- When I cast it and what the conditions were
- How I raised and sealed the energy
- How long the spell stayed active
- How easy it was to repeat

Keep it simple. Sometimes removing an ingredient makes a spell stronger. Over time, you'll start to notice which combinations feel clean and clear—and which ones get muddy. If you change something, be specific. Don't write "added more rosemary." Write "used three sprigs instead of one to strengthen boundaries," and then see what that shift brings.

You'll start to notice patterns. Some timings feel more powerful. Certain pairings amplify each other.

I remember my friend, Mia's, first original jar. She made it for her mom who was anxious before a big event. She used traditional herbs but added coffee grounds too—something that felt tied to her friend's routine and energy. The mix was simple, intentional and real. That's why it worked.

That's the heart of refining your magic. Stay curious. Trust what feels right. And write it down. You're not trying to reinvent anything. You're shaping something that carries your voice, your insight, your care.

CHAPTER 8

The Quiet Work After the Spell

A spell jar isn't finished when you seal the lid. That's when the care begins. Think of it like a garden. You don't plant something and walk away. You check in. You feel the changes and notice when something starts to shift or fade. That's how it is with spell jars. Like any living thing, they're tended, supported, or taken apart when the time comes.

When I first started, no one told me that. I had to learn by feel. I remember one jar I made for protection. At first, it pulsed with energy, then, slowly, something shifted. The salt inside had clumped. The herbs turned dull and lifeless. It didn't feel right anymore. But I didn't rush to throw it out, I sat with it. I placed it in my lap and listened. That's when I began to understand that spellwork doesn't stop when the candle goes out. It's something you live with, care for, and release when the time comes.

A friend told me about a prosperity jar she made while looking for work. Months later, after a promotion and a raise, she noticed the honey had thickened and the herbs had faded. She didn't toss it in the bin. She took a breath, gave thanks, and waited for the new moon. She then emptied the jar slowly, threw the herbs into the compost, and the glass into the recycling. What she couldn't reuse, she buried. That quiet act said more than words. It marked the end of something, and the beginning of what came next.

This is part of the practice. You make spells, tend to them, listen closely, and let them go when their time is done.

In this chapter, I'll show you how I care for my spell jars, what signs I look for, and the small rituals I use when it's time to release them. Let your rhythm emerge and stay with the work until it's truly done.

Like a garden, your spell jars need tending. Regular care keeps their energy clear and their purpose strong. Over time, you'll learn to notice when a jar needs attention. Sometimes the signs are physical. Sometimes they're more intuitive. Either way, they're part of the quiet conversation between you and your magic.

You might notice the signs physically first. Things that once felt settled start to shift. Look for:

- Mold or cloudiness
- Herbs that have lost their color
- Salt that clumps or gathers moisture
- Honey that crystallizes

- Wax seals that crack or loosen

These changes aren't about age or wear. They often point to energy that's grown stagnant, or to a spell that's finished its work. When a jar starts to fall apart, the energy it holds can start to drift. Like an open circle in ritual, it breaks the flow.

Magical signs can be quieter. A jar that once felt strong might now feel heavy or flat. You might find yourself thinking about it often, dreaming about it, or feeling the urge to go check on it. Those nudges mean something.

Pay attention to:

- A dull or muddled energy
- A sense that the spell has lost direction
- Unsettled feelings when you pass by
- Repeated dreams or thoughts about the same jar
- A clear pull to revisit or change it

These kinds of feelings often show up before anything physical does. Listening early can save you from letting something go stale. One thing that helps me is checking my jars once a month during the waning moon. That's when I slow down and reflect. I look at each jar and ask:

- Has anything changed?
- Does this still feel connected to the purpose I made it for?
- Is it working—or has it faded?
- Is anything calling me to do it now?

Not every change is a problem. Sometimes it means the spell has done its job. If a prosperity jar begins to harden or fade after your money worries ease, that might be the jar saying, "I'm finished."

My journal tracks these shifts. I write down what the jar looks like, how it feels, and what's happening in my life around it. Over time, this becomes a map of your practice—alive, changing, honest.

When it's time to act, keep it simple. You might recharge the jar under the moon. You might replace a few herbs or cleanse the whole thing. And sometimes, you'll retire it. Thank it for what it did. Let it go with care.

Your magic isn't meant to sit still. It grows with you. When you stay close to your jars, you stay close to your craft. And that connection deepens every time you choose to listen.

Like any living thing, a spell jar needs care. It's not something you set and forget. With regular attention—both physical and energetic—you help the magic stay clear and active.

Cleansing clears away anything that's built up or doesn't belong. You might pass the jar through herb smoke like rosemary or sage. You could use sound—bells, singing bowls, even a simple hum. Leaving the jar in moonlight works too. Choose what fits your space. If smoke isn't an option, light and sound can do the job. What matters is your focus while you do it.

Charging brings the energy back up. You can sit with the jar and meditate on your intention. Or work with a crystal, a candle, something simple and steady. I often use color magic here—green for money, white for peace, black for protection. I let the candle burn beside the jar while holding the goal in mind.

For spells that last longer, it helps to strengthen them now and then. I "feed" the jar—maybe with a pinch of herb, a drop of oil, or a note with an updated intention. I try to time it with a moon phase that matches the work.

You'll know when a jar needs your attention. The liquid might turn cloudy. The colors may fade. Or the energy might just feel heavy or dull. Trust your instincts. If it feels off, it probably is.

Each time you tend to a jar, write it down. What you did, when you did it, and how the energy shifted after. This builds your understanding over time. And if you don't have tools to hand, don't worry. Visualization works. So does intention. You don't need anything elaborate—just presence and respect for the work you're doing.

Like any sacred tool or space, spell jars thrive with care. I learned this the hard way—one of my first jars, a protection spell, sat untouched for months. When I finally checked in, it felt flat. The salt had clumped, the herbs dulled. The spell hadn't failed, but it needed me to show up again.

Your jars will ask for your attention too. Not loudly—but through small changes you'll start to notice as your practice deepens.

I tend to refresh mine when:

- The spell feels weaker or less clear
- The energy around the jar feels off or stale
- The contents start to look different—herbs fade, salt cakes, honey hardens
- A meaningful moment comes around, like a new moon, a seasonal shift, or a fresh chapter in my life

Step 1: Observe and Listen

Before doing anything, I pause and sit with the jar. I ask myself: does it still feel alive? Has it shifted? Sometimes, a jar that once buzzed with protection feels quiet. Or a prosperity jar starts to feel blocked. These subtle changes often tell me it's time to renew.

Step 2: Cleanse the Energy

Then I clear any stagnant energy. What I use depends on the jar:

- **Smoke** — rosemary or bay leaves are my go-to
- **Sound** — bells, clapping, even humming works in a pinch
- **Nature** — moonlight for protection, midday sun for prosperity, fresh air or a stream for healing work

Step 3: Feed the Spell

Next, I add something fresh:

- A pinch of herb, a drop of oil, a small charm or token
- Something symbolic that reconnects me to the jar's purpose

Don't worry about having the "right" ingredients. I've used basil from my kitchen and a button when I didn't have a coin. What matters is the meaning behind it.

Step 4: Realign Your Intention

This is the heart of it. I hold the jar, close my eyes, and reconnect with why I made it in the first place. I let the memory rise, visualize what I'm calling in, and speak the intention again, clear and steady.

If I can't add anything physical (like when I'm traveling or sharing space), I focus on breathwork, visualization, or a quiet affirmation. That's enough.

Adapting by Purpose

Each jar needs something a little different:

- **Protection** — I might add a pinch of black salt or reinforce the boundary in my mind

- **Prosperity** — A fresh coin, a thank-you, a reminder of what's flowing in
- **Healing** — A clear quartz or simply placing my hands over the jar with a quiet prayer for ease

I try to jot down what I did and how the jar felt after. Over time, patterns appear. You'll start to see what your magic responds to, how long things last, and how your practice changes with you.

Letting go of a spell jar matters just as much as making one. It marks the end of the spell's cycle. It's a way of returning energy with care, focus and thanks.

So how do you know when it's time?

- The spell has done what you asked
- You feel, deep down, that it's complete
- The jar starts to show signs—mold, leaking, a loosened seal

Once you've decided to release it, think about what kind of spell it was. Each type asks for its own kind of goodbye.

- A protection jar can be buried at the edge of your home to hold the energy in place
- A banishing or release jar belongs far from home—at a crossroads or by flowing water where it can move on
- Abundance jars often like to be buried under a healthy plant, somewhere the energy can keep growing
- Memorial or remembrance jars should be released with care—buried or scattered somewhere that holds meaning

Before you dispose of anything, take the jar apart.

- Crystals or charms can be cleansed and reused
- Herbs and other organic bits can be composted or buried
- Paper can be burned, if that's something you work with
- Glass jars should be washed in salt water or passed through purifying herbs

Then, make space for a small ritual. Clear the area. Thank the energy that supported you. Let it go with focus and respect. If you're working in nature, be thoughtful. Don't bury plastic or anything that won't break down. Don't throw salty or toxic items into rivers or lakes. If you're unsure, check the local rules first.

And if you don't have easy access to outdoor space, that's fine.

- Use a plant pot on your windowsill
- Compost anything biodegradable
- Rely on intention and visualization to guide the release

Letting go isn't the end. It's part of the rhythm. It opens space for what comes next. It keeps the energy in your craft moving and alive.

Letting go of a spell jar can be just as meaningful as casting it. When you take time to release your work with care, you close the loop in a way that respects both your craft and the natural world.

As witches, we're part of nature—not separate from it. That means we have a responsibility to return what we've used in a way that doesn't cause harm. Eco-conscious disposal isn't about perfection. It's about thoughtfulness.

I've found that the best time to think about disposal is before making the spell. Ask yourself: what will I do with this when it's done? Choose ingredients and containers you can release or reuse with care. I often use old kitchen jars, they're easy to clean, they save money, and they already carry the energy of daily life.

Herbs, flowers, and other natural elements can be composted or buried, as long as they don't contain salt, wax, or synthetic oils. This way, you return your materials to the earth in a nourishing way. It's part of the cycle. What once carried your intention can now support new growth.

You can reuse crystals and charms if they've been properly cleansed. I like to give mine a rinse in salt water or leave them out overnight under the moon. You can try melting down wax from natural candles to make into new ones.

If something isn't reusable or compostable, don't panic. Dispose of it through regular waste collection—but always close the spell first. Cleanse the jar. Say thank you. Release its energy with intention.

Some traditional practices suggest burying whole jars. For protective or banishing work, that made sense in the past—but if the jar includes plastic, salt, or anything that won't break down, it's better to adapt. We can honor tradition without damaging the land.

I always perform a small ritual before releasing a jar. I thank the energies, speak my release aloud, and pause to acknowledge the work that's been done. This moment of closure helps me let go with clarity.

To keep your practice aligned with the earth:

- Use jars you can clean and reuse
- Choose natural ingredients that return safely to the soil
- Separate your components before disposal
- Avoid burying anything non-biodegradable
- Check local compost and recycling guidelines

- Write down what worked, so you can build on it next time

When I started paying more attention to how I let go of my spell jars, I noticed a shift. My work felt cleaner. My space felt lighter. And I began to see disposal not as an afterthought, but as an offering.

This kind of stewardship doesn't limit your craft—it deepens it. By taking care of the land that supports our work, we become better witches and better caretakers of the world we live in.

Your Practice Starts Here

Authors Note

Jar magic isn't about filling containers. It's about shaping intention with care and in a way that feels real to you. Every jar you make is part of something bigger. It's a practice that will grow over time and connect you to something older than yourself.

Throughout this book, we've looked at how simple ingredients can become something powerful when they're chosen with care. You've seen how jars can protect, heal, and invite change, not because they follow a strict formula, but because they reflect your intention. We've explored both traditional methods and modern needs, and how the two can sit side by side without losing their power.

What matters most now is that you keep going. Let your practice evolve. Pay attention to what works. Trust your instincts, respect the craft, and stay open to learning as you go. Magic doesn't need to be perfect to be meaningful.

Showing up and being present is the real work. However you choose to use jar spells from here, let it be something that supports your life and brings you closer to your values.

Bibliography

Peru Explorer. (2024, November 8). *Ancient Peru Wizardry: Sacred Rituals & Magic*. Peru Explorer. https://www.peru-explorer.com/ancient-peru-wizardry-sacred-rituals-magic.htm

Siegel, M. (2023). *Spell jars for the modern witch: A practical guide to crafting spell jars for abundance, luck, protection, and more.* Ulysses Press.

Lucci, G.. (2023, March 24). *Whistling Vessels - Magical Mysteries.* Shamans Market. https://www.shamansmarket.com/blogs/musings/whistling-vessels-magical-mysteries

Kane, A.. (2023). *Protection Spells: An Enchanting Spell Book to Clear Negative Energy*. Scribd. https://www.scribd.com/document/709292195/Protection-Spells-an-Enchanting-Spell-Book-to-Clear-Negative-Energy-Aurora-Kane-Z-Library

Bedell C. L.. (2023, January 02). *6 Simple Jar Spells Using Common Household Objects*. Llewellyn Worldwide. https://www.llewellyn.com/journal/article/3073

BWS. (2023, January 1). *How Container Magic Spells Work*. Black Witch Coven. https://blackwitchcoven.com/how-container-magic-spells-work/

Shayne, M.. (2025, March 02). *How to Make a Witch's Bottle*. Bliss Blog. https://blissblog.substack.com/p/how-to-make-a-witchs-bottle

Savannah. (2019, July). *Consecration*. Black Witch Coven. https://blackwitchcoven.com/how-tos/consecration/

Brown, A.S.. (2021, October). *A Ritual for Blessing Magical Tools*. Pagan Song. https://pagansong.com/a-ritual-for-blessing-magical-tools/

Arkadian, A.. (2024, June 20). *Alchemy: The Three Principles (Tria Prima)*. Aerik Arkadian. https://aerikarkadian.com/2024/06/20/alchemy-the-three-principles-tria-prima/

[1]Goodson, M.. (2020, July 22). *The Stoppered Vessel*. The Zen Gateway. https://www.thezengateway.com/culture/the-alchemy-of-transformation-the-stoppered-vessel

Blooding, Frankie. (2024, February 17). *Creating Sacred Spaces: Witchcraft in Everyday Life*. Frankie Jo's Storyland. https://substack.com/home/post/p-141764562

Baker E. M.. (2024, November 13). *A Witches Guide to Sacred Space*. City Witch. https://www.citywitch.co.uk/a-witches-guide-to-sacred-space/

Townsend, E.. (2025, February 26). *Witch in the Workplace: Part 1*. Rebel Soul ⋆ High Vibe Badass. https://substack.com/home/post/p-157665220

Regan S.. (2023, June 15). *How To Make Your Own Spell Jar For Love, Protection, Money & More*. mindbodygreen. https://www.mindbodygreen.com/articles/spell-jars

Unity. (2023, March 15). *Ritual to Consecrate Magical Tools*. Kitchen Witch Hearth. https://www.kitchenwitchhearth.net/post/ritual-to-consecrate-magical-tools-by-unity

Whisper in the Wood. (2022, September). *Craft Your Own Magical Jars*. Enchanted Living Magazine. https://enchantedlivingmagazine.com/craft-your-own-magical-jars/

Burgess, L.. (2023, March 28). *The Complete Guide to Spell Jars - Witchcraft Basics*. Backyard Banshee. https://backyardbanshee.com/witchcraft/spell-jars/

Witchcraft Emporium. (2023, October 15). *The Four Elements in Witchcraft: A Guide to Elemental Magic Correspondences*. Witchcraft Emporium. https://www.witchcraft-emporium.com/post/the-four-elements-in-witchcraft-a-guide-to-elemental-magic-correspondences

Baker E. M.. (2025, February 19). *A Comprehensive Guide to Magical Correspondences*. City Witch. https://www.citywitch.co.uk/magical-correspondences/

Hart, A.. (2025, February 26). *The Complete Beginners Guide To Herbs For Witchcraft*. The Occult Witch. https://theoccultwitch.com/blog/the-complete-beginners-guide-to-herbs-for-witchcraft

Art of the Root. (2025, April 17). *Herbs, Roots, and Mistletoe: A Guide to Plant Spirit Magic*. Art of the Root. https://artoftheroot.com/blogs/spells-and-rituals/herbs-roots-and-mistletoe-a-guide-to-plant-spirit-magic

Wolfe S. E.. (2022, October 10). *Witchy DIYs: Crafting Spell Jars for Your Desires*. Green Witch Living. https://blog.greenwitchliving.com/crafting-spell-jars-for-your-desires/

Eclectic Charge. (2021, July 18). *Spellwork: Spell Jars II - Creativity, Safe Travel, and Psychic Spell Jars*. Eclectic Charge. https://eclecticcharge.com/spellwork-spell-jars-ii/

Black, Bec. (2023, May 19). *A History of Witch Bottles and Spell Jars*. Witchcraft Spells Magick. https://witchcraftspellsmagick.com/blogs/witch-studies/witch-bottles

n.d.) https://the-witches-path.com/lunar-magic/

Spells8. (2025, February 01). *Full Moon Correspondences: The Essence of Lunar Energy*. Spells8. https://spells8.com/full-moon-correspondences/

Uhl, C.. (2023, December 16). *Winter Solstice & Yule Spell Jar for Rebirth*. Cassie Uhl. https://www.cassieuhl.com/blog/winter-solstice-yule-spell-jar-for-rebirth

Patterson, R.. (2016, May 16). *Magical Jar Spells*. Rachel Patterson. https://www.rachelpatterson.co.uk/single-post/magical-jar-spells

Mystical Zodiac Shop. (2024, March 14). *Spring Witchcraft Spells and Rituals to Awaken the Season's Magic*. Mystical Zodiac Shop. https://mysticalzodiacshop.com/blogs/news/spring-witchcraft-spells-and-rituals-to-awaken-the-season-s-magic

Harker, E.. (2024, January 25). *Waning Crescent Moon // Energy + Rituals*. The Magick Makers. https://themagickmakers.com/blog/waning-crescent-moon-energy-rituals

The Hoodwitch. (2023, September 15). *Living By The Moon*. The Hoodwitch. https://www.thehoodwitch.com/timing-spells-by-the-moon

Niriksha. (2023, April 11). *Herbs for Protection Spell Jar | Best Ingredients & Recipes*. Brahmas. https://brahmas.co/blog/herbs-for-protection-spell-jar/

O'Neill, H.. (2023, October 23). *How To Make A Spell Jar*. Suburban Witchery. https://www.suburbanwitchery.com/blog/how-to-make-a-spell-jar

Jol. (2024, February 6). *Protection spell jar*. Lemon8. https://www.lemon8-app.com/@soulnamedjol/7376097909202452997?region=us

Galerie R Berry. (2024, April 5). *When Your Spell Jar Breaks: Understanding and Navigating the Path Forward*. Galerie RBerry. https://www.galerierberry.com/blog-spiritual-musings/when-your-spell-jar-breaks-understanding-and-navigating-the-path-forward

Art of the Root. (2025, March 06). *How to Craft Honey Jars & Witch Bottles for Love & Protection*. Art of the Root. https://artoftheroot.com/blogs/spells-and-rituals/how-to-craft-honey-jars-witch-bottles-for-love-protection

Lancs Green Witch. (2024, December). *Prosperity Jar Spell: How to Manifest Abundance in Your Home*. Lancs Green Witch. https://www.lancsgreenwitch.co.uk/prosperity-jar-spell-manifest-abundance-in-your-home/

Eclectic Charge. (2021, July 25). *Spellwork: Spell Jars I*. Eclectic Charge. https://eclecticcharge.com/spellwork-spell-jars-i/

Brakels, B.. (2023, April 13). *New Moon Spells*. Tragic Beautiful. https://www.tragicbeautiful.com/en-us/blogs/book-of-spells/new-moon-spells

Brakels, B.. (2023, March 27). *Full Moon Spells*. Tragic Beautiful. https://www.tragicbeautiful.com/en-us/blogs/book-of-spells/full-moon-spells

Baker, E. M.. (2023, July 22). *Crafting powerful spell jars: A city witch guide*. City Witch. https://www.citywitch.co.uk/how-to-make-a-personalised-spell-jar/

X, Melanie. (2024, August 26). *How to Make a Spell Jar*. Tragic Beautiful. https://www.tragicbeautiful.com/en-us/blogs/book-of-spells/how-to-make-a-spell-jar

Sidney Eileen. (2020, September 1). *Ethical Baneful Magic for all Skill and Experience Levels*. Sidney Eileen. https://sidneyeileen.com/2020/09/01/ethical-baneful-magic-for-all-skill-and-experience-levels/

Sunnolia, E.. (2023, October 14). *Spellwork and Witchcraft Ethics*. Cassie Uhl. https://www.cassieuhl.com/blog/spellwork-and-witchcraft-ethics/

J Southern Studio. (2023, July 11). *Spellwork Sessions: Protection Spell Jar for Banishing and Binding*. JSouthernStudio. https://www.jsouthernstudio.com/blogs/esotericinsights/spellwork-sundays-protection-spell-jar

Wolf, Metztli. (2024, March 28). *Souring Jar Spells: A Hoodoo Expert's DIY Guide*. Revolutionary Mystic. https://revolutionarymystic.com/blogs/spellwork-astrology-wolfdogs/souring-jar-spells-a-hoodoo-experts-diy-guide

Art of the Root. (2024, June 12). *How to Create A Honey Jar Spell for Love or Success*. Art of the Root. https://artoftheroot.com/blogs/spells-and-rituals/how-to-create-a-honey-jar-spell-for-love-or-success

Cowley, L.. (2021, September 09). *How to dispose of a spell jar*. The Crystal and Wellness Warehouse. https://www.thecrystalandwellnesswarehouse.com.au/blogs/news/how-to-dispose-of-a-spell-jar

Patterson, R.. (2020, August 25). *Ending and Disposing of Spells.* Patheos. https://www.patheos.com/blogs/beneaththemoon/2020/08/ending-and-disposing-of-spells/

Goddess Enchantments. (2020, December 12). *Safely Disposing Of Spell & Ritual Left Overs.* Goddess Enchantments. https://www.goddess-enchantments.co.uk/how-to-dispose-of-spell-ingredients-and-left-over-materials.html

Other titles by Maren Ashford

The Spiritual Witch Series

- The Spiritual Witch: A complete Guide to Modern Witchcraft and Magical Practice for Beginners
- Jar Spells for the Spiritual Witch: A Step-by-Step Guide to Creating Your Own Spells for Protection, Prosperity, & Peace
- Moon Witch: Ancient Wisdom and Modern Practices for Lunar-Powered Magic
- Moon Goddesses – coming 2026

www.ingramcontent.com/pod-product-compliance
Lightning Source LLC
LaVergne TN
LVHW050317160826
845677LV00014B/3437